Native American Flute Craft

Ancient to Modern

C.S. Fuqua

Published by
WindPoem Creative
in association with
Cooperative Ink

Original photography by Tegan Fuqua. Cover image combines photographs of the Organ Mountains National Monument at dawn, an early flute by C.S. Fuqua, and one step in the flute crafting process.

This book is an outgrowth of *The Native American Flute: Myth, History, Craft* by C.S. Fuqua, its purpose to provide more detailed instruction in the crafting and care of Native American flutes.

First Edition

ISBN-13: 978-1514675564
ISBN-10: 1514675560

For the love of music
and the people who make it...

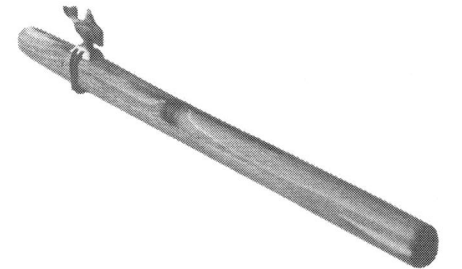

Contents

Acknowledgements

Many thanks to the readers who've provided feedback on *The Native American Flute: Myth, History, Craft.* Your input and suggestions have been instrumental in writing and designing this book to better address the needs and interests of potential flute makers.

I'm indebted to the craftspeople and musicians I've met over the years, who have generously shared their knowledge on crafting, history, playing, and more. Many thanks to master flute maker Jack Thomas, who unselfishly provided straightforward information when I began crafting flutes. Without his instruction and suggestions via mail and email, I would not have developed the skills as quickly. I'm also grateful to Michael Graham Allen for making the extraordinary cedar flute that hooked me on that long ago day in the Alabama flea market.

A big thank you to author, musician, and good friend Dick Claassen for *insisting* this book be written. Without his unyielding encouragement and assurances of vast wealth beyond all measure, not to mention fame, the book would never have been produced. Now, Dick, about that wealth and fame…

Thank you, as always, to Bonnie and Tegan for their support and assistance throughout the research, crafting, and writing of this book.

And thank *you* for purchasing *Native American Flute Craft*. I hope it serves you well.

Preface

If you've read *The Native American Flute: Myth, History, Craft*, some of the information here will be familiar, especially in the preface and first chapter. I've borrowed bits and pieces from *Myth, History, Craft* to provide a summary of flute-related history and mythology—some needed background to precede the crafting sections of this book. For those who are interested primarily in history and mythology, *Myth, History, Craft* explores the Native American flute's development and romanticization more completely and has a limited section on crafting. This book is designed to provide in-depth, specific crafting instructions, greatly expanding the instructions provided in *Myth, History, Craft*—which leads me to the words *thank you*. Yes, thank you for allowing me to share with you my experience and knowledge in crafting Native American flutes.

Although rumors persist among some of my relatives that our direct ancestry includes members of the Creek (Muscogee) Indian nation, DNA analy-

sis has proved otherwise. I claim no Native American heritage, and I am not associated with or a member of any Native American tribe. I am, however, a full-time writer and part-time hobbyist woodworker with a keen interest in music, native history, and Native American flutes.

As a writer, I spend a good portion of my day in a room with only books, a computer, and an internet connection. Before the computer, I utilized a typewriter when I wasn't researching at the local library. It's possible I accomplished more work then than I do now with the internet at my fingertips. My spouse has often told me I need to get out more—"Take a walk, breathe fresh air, and wear sunscreen!" After all, neither typewriter nor computer can substitute for direct understanding. A writer can wax poetically about walking in rain or sun, crafting a piece of furniture or a flute, or basking in a gulf breeze, but words on paper or a computer screen cannot rival the actual experience.

So I did as she suggested some

twenty-five years ago and began to explore the Native American flute. At first, my interest was limited strictly to listening to the performances of others. Then, by chance, I played a flute.

I became aware of the Native American flute during the 1980s through the recordings of artists such as R. Carolos Nakai and the Coyote Oldman duo. A fan of indigenous instruments, especially flutes, from around the world, I didn't see or hear a Native American flute in person until the early 1990s, when I happened upon a booth in a North Alabama flea market. The proprietor offered customers a plethora of "new age" products, including instruments and CD music from around the world. The Native American flute, due to its indigenous origin and use primarily for ambient background music, had been labeled as *new age*, and the proprietor stocked a few native flutes in his inventory, each in the key of F# and made of eastern aromatic red cedar. By whatever stroke of happenstance the universe occasionally orchestrates, the flutes on hand had been crafted by Michael Graham Allen, founding member and flautist of Coyote Oldman, the duo whose music I was most familiar with at the time. (Some twenty years later, I would correspond with Mr. Allen while

researching and writing a book on native Alabama musicians.)

As a full-time writer, I was then and remain frugal when it comes to money. Most full-time writers, at least in my experience, don't maintain vast funds for discretionary, impulse purchases, especially items that exceed the "fun" budget for the next few weeks combined. Even so, after putting that flute to my lips and producing such a mellow, soulful, beautiful sound, it was difficult, to say the very least, to put it down and walk away. Something about its tone reached straight into my being, grabbed a piece of my soul, and would not let go. I forced myself to place it back on the counter and leave, but the experience had planted the seed of determination for me to own such a flute someday.

I thus began a journey of research, learning, experimentation, and exploration that would lead to dozens of failed attempts before successfully crafting a playable, satisfying Native American flute. Years and hundreds of flutes later came the writing and publication of *The Native American Flute: Myth, History, Craft*, a book that details the native flute's mythology and true history, with a limited how-to section for hobbyist woodcrafters on making both ancient and modern versions.

The Native American Flute

Myth
History
Craft

C. S. Fuqua

So why have I now written a book specifically on crafting?

Since publication of *The Native American Flute: Myth, History, Craft*, I've continued to research all aspects of the instrument, further developing my skills through trial and error, not always with great success, as you'll see later. For the past couple of years, native flute musician and dear friend Dick Claassen has been encouraging—nay, *nagging*—me to write a more detailed how-to book on crafting, a book with instructions designed for beginner through advanced level flute crafters. Such a book, he insisted, should include not only calculations for making flutes of any size and from various materials, but also instructions with specific measurements, requiring no independent calculation by the crafter. The book, he pointed out repeatedly, should incorporate lots of photographs to illustrate the steps involved.

I took his advice.

For better or worse, *Native American Flute Craft* is the result.

If you'd like to hear some of the flutes made during the writing of this book, please visit my website at http://csfuqua.weebly.com for links to the CD series, *WindPoem ~ Native American Flute Meditations*.

Note: *Certain instructions are repeated in different sections to eliminate the need to flip back and forth between chapters. Also, fetish, bird, block, and air block are used interchangeably in the text since the terms refer to the same flute component. Labium and sound hole are also terms that refer to a single component and are used interchangeably.*

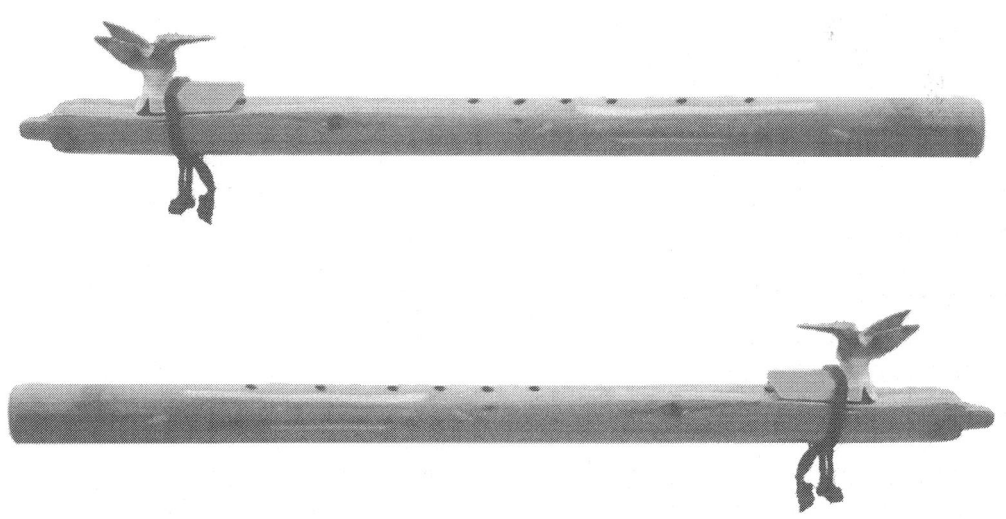

Chapter One

Back Story

Since the mid-1980s, interest in crafting the Native American flute has grown steadily. Through the mid-1990s, however, reliable, specific instruction on crafting the flute was almost as scarce to come by as reliable accounts of its history and development. Since the internet was in its infancy, potential flute makers and people interested in the instrument's history couldn't simply log on to access instant information. Furthermore, the only how-to publications at the time were randomly available, self-published, mail-order, fold-and-staple booklets that offered primarily personal philosophy on the flute, life, and the physics of sound—mystical musings well beyond the interest of someone like me, trying to locate simple instruction on crafting a basic folk instrument. Specifically, I wanted to know how to make a wooden cylinder with the standard bore size, where to drill air, sound, and finger holes, and how to shape the labi-

um for sound. I wanted dimensions, a tools list, a you-can-do-it set of instructions laid out simply, understandably, without clutter, without politics, without mysticism, and, mostly, without complicated calculations based on physics and air turbulence, concepts and mathematics I would never comprehend.

I made dozens of trips to public and university libraries in search of whatever scrap of understandable information I could locate on the flute, from its history to mythology to craft. Some of the most useful information came in tidbits buried in the pages of children's books and in popular interest books that topically explored Native American history. Still, no publication I could locate provided information specific and detailed enough to enable someone to develop the ability to craft a playable instrument. Over time, I located a few crafters from around the U.S., but either the quality

Woodworking projects like those pictured here helped me to develop skills useful in crafting Native American flutes. Also pictured are a few of my early flutes, crafted from naturally downed southern pine and aromatic cedar. Most of my early flutes went to friends in the U.S., Japan, and Australia.

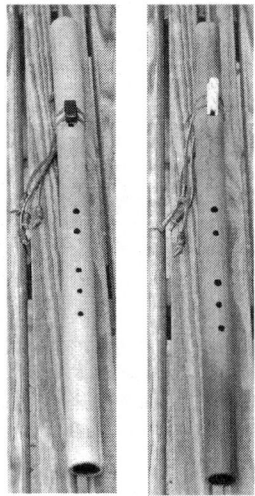

of flutes wasn't worth the price, or the superb quality of an instrument demanded a price I couldn't afford. So I decided to experiment, based on the scant information I had gleaned from library books and anything I might learn from the self-published pamphlets I decided to order.

I was already a hobbyist woodworker, crafting projects that included furniture and children's toys designed more for functionality than beauty. Although I'd never attempted to make a musical instrument, I assumed that it wouldn't be *that* difficult. What did I know?

I returned to the flea market and examined the flute by Michael Graham Allen more closely. Its construction appeared straightforward enough. With time and experimentation, I concluded, I could develop a method for crafting a playable instrument.

The pamphlets arrived. Although lacking in instruction aimed at the beginner, the pamphlets provided more usable information than I'd been able to locate elsewhere. Intent on developing a standard method by which to craft, I began building flutes, but early attempts failed miserably. Even so, I learned a lot about crafting a functional fetish, routing wood, and shaping barrels, air and sound chambers, and sound holes.

As the internet expanded, increasing access to flute makers around the world as more discovered and utilized the new medium as an effective marketing tool, I contacted a few seasoned crafters, including Jack Thomas, a gifted flute maker of museum quality instruments. A generous and extraordinarily talented wood carver, he provided a full-scale drawing for making an F# Native American flute, using a one-inch diameter PVC pipe. Another maker

suggested a basic calculation to determine placement of the fourth finger hole. The other holes could be determined, he said, by the width of maker's thumb, but adjustments would be needed from flute to flute. From that method evolved a simple math equation and percentages for calculating finger hole placement more precisely on flutes of any key and physical size, eliminating both guesswork based on thumb width and convoluted physics equations that rely on strict measurements of bore and length, air turbulence, and other factors.

At first, I suspected the percentage method might not work in many cases, but, to my delight, the formula and percentages have proved extremely reliable, although some tweaking can improve placement in keys above A and below C#. I recently compared two of my F# flutes, one crafted about twenty-two years ago, the other only a year ago, both by utilizing the percentage method. One is bamboo with a 15/16-inch bore. The other is PVC with a 3/4-inch bore. Although the bamboo flute is slightly shorter than the PVC flute, the percentages and formula (detailed later in the crafting chapters) resulted in correct finger hole placement on each—two flutes of different sizes, playing the same key and notes in tune.

Assimilation

While researching and developing a reliable crafting technique, I became well aware of the mythology that overshadows the instrument's true history. The flute is popularly known as the Native American *love* flute—in many cases, that's the *only* way it's identified—a celebrated notion that the flute was developed solely as a tool for seduction, an instrument that would, in the hands of a desiring young man, hold mystical sway over women. That extraordinarily misogynistic European view did not fit well with what I already knew about indigenous cultures of the Americas, especially North American cultures that were matriarchal before the European invasion.

Most Americans today, including Native Americans, thanks to the systematic destruction of native culture and obliteration of native history through assimilation in the name of God and country, perpetuate a stereotypical view of native women, a view created by early prejudiced, ethnocentric European accounts of Native American cultures, accounts that have been exacerbated through the years by the derogatory, historically deceptive depiction of Native Americans in Hollywood western movies, popular literature, and racially biased history taught in American schools, depictions and perceptions that persist due to an incomprehensible unwillingness to admit fact.

If we Americans know anything, it's how to rewrite history to sanitize truth and promote a particular point of view. Consider the current political movement to abolish history courses that explore both positive *and* negative aspects of American history, to fill history classrooms with books that, instead, exaggerate the country's assets, real and imagined, and ignore its transgressions both at home and abroad. The so-called representatives of the free world and proponents of free speech pushing this agenda believe that anything they deem negative or contrary to their view of what is and isn't *American* should be forbidden in education, that students should be fed a concoction of half-baked nonsense, conspiracy theories, and polit-

ical ideology that promotes ethnocentrism and superiority. American history texts, according to these political ideologues, should promote their party's political talking points, revision of facts, and just plain boloney, no matter how extreme, no matter how fictitious, no matter how harmful to the nation or world at large. The movement, pandering to fear and prejudice, has met strong opposition in some states, while other states have gleefully embraced it.

European demonization of indigenous people in the Americas may have resulted more from fear of cultural influence than anything else. Despite their technological and scientific inferiority, most native cultures were more socially evolved than the culture of European invaders. Indigenous societies posed a sociological threat to the patriarchal mentality of Europeans. Matriarchal culture centered its spiritual beliefs in an all-inclusive *Sacred Circle*, asserting that life itself is a circle in which *everything* is connected and occupies purpose, that animals, insects, plants, rocks— *everything*—deserves respect and honor for its place within the circle. Further, that respect and honor within native tribes extended to *all* individuals, embracing and celebrating a wide latitude in personal diversity, from homosexual males and females to nurturing, pacifist males and assertive, decisive women. All were accepted and honored within the group rather than demeaned and punished for their differences. Indigenous cultures focused on social responsibility and acceptance, not social denial and individual conformity.

Immigrant missionaries and explorers, folks who were definitely *not* the best choice to interpret, understand, or judge Native American culture, provided early written accounts of American

Indian life to the masses back in Europe. Bolstered by an abundance of sanctimonious superiority, their accounts perpetrated a horrendously detailed picture of *savages* kidnapping European women who ventured too far from camp, enslaving them as white *squaws*. The word *squaw* carried and continues to carry many connotations, most derogatory. A *squaw*, according to those who argue the word's a compliment, is a woman who's strong, independent, and guiding. Based on its use in film and literature, however, the word has been saturated with negative connotations to become a tool to denigrate native women, defining them as weak, dependent, ineffectual, and property. By portraying indigenous women as inferior rather than equal to their male counterparts, Europeans chipped away at the matriarchal base upon which native societies had been built, replacing it with the patriarchal structure of European society, its goal to dispense civility, social harmony, and Christian redemption to the evil barbarians inhabiting the Americas.

It was a huge undertaking. After all, native societies valued women as much as they valued men, perhaps even more so. A family's ancestral line was traced through the mother, not the father. Women participated equally in decisions affecting the village. Some women fought in battles alongside their male counterparts. Men tended to domestic and village chores alongside their female counterparts. In many indigenous cultures, women were believed to possess the ability to dream power for themselves, power that could be utilized in areas such as medicine, food gathering, and food preparation. Although a man headed a clan in everyday decision making, the clan mother chose that leader and could oust him if she deemed

him a failure in carrying out his duties.

Native women didn't need to wage decades of protest and civil battle to gain the right to vote. They had always possessed that right. Every person counted, and treaties with outside parties required support by at least three-fourths of all voters and, in many cases, three-fourths of all mothers. If the community's women became dissatisfied with the chief, they could impeach him. Impeachment was seldom pursued, however, because women commonly served in advisory positions to the chief and assisted him in managing village affairs. And when the grave possibility of war emerged, women could veto the option.

Native American creation myths further emphasize the importance of women. In an Iroquois tale, for example, Woman Who Dreams Dreams has a dream about a great tree that sinks through the ground, creating a hole through which she falls and eventually lands in water where sea creatures and birds assist her in creating the planet earth. In a similar version, Skywoman falls through the hole and is placed upon a great turtle's back by a flock of geese. The turtle grows in shape and size to form earth, and Skywoman gives birth to a daughter whose children propagate the human race. (These myths and others are explored more fully in *The Native American Flute: Myth, History, Craft*.)

Gender Defining

Defeating Native Americans and taking their property, Europeans relegated the various cultures to reservations where missionaries and other immigrant do-gooders systematically destroyed native culture and history, forcibly assimilating American Indians into a European, Judeo-Christian mindset. The power, equality, and authority that native women had once possessed disintegrated. Undermining and ultimately destroying the native way of life involved the erosion and elimination of all that was honorable and sacred, from the historical role of women within a tribe to the elimination of the various nations' myths and religions. All that had been *native* was reinvented and recast through the European worldview. Native reality became western fancy, fancy that included elements such as the Native American flute. Even though the flute had been an integral part of native social life, used in everything from simple entertainment and courting to fertility celebrations and rites, played by men and women alike, the only myth to be retained and promoted was the courting myth, masculinizing the instrument and further denigrating and marginalizing women.

Early descriptions of the flute are exemplified by artist George Catlin's 1832 account, in which he suggests that the flute is not a product of native culture at all, but "would seem to have been borrowed, in part, from the civilized world. I often heard this instrument, called the Winnebago courting flute, and was credibly informed by traders and others in those regions that the young men of that tribe meet with success, oftentimes, in wooing their sweethearts with its simple notes, which they blow for hours together, and from day to day, from the bank of some stream—some favorite rock or log on which they are seated, near to the wigwam which contains the object of their tender passion until her soul is touched,

and she responds by some welcome signal, that she is ready to repay the young Orpheus for his pains with the gift of her hand and her heart."

Other accounts of the flute have luckily survived, despite the European campaign to romanticize the instrument. These accounts underscore the fact that the flute was and remains far more than a courting instrument used only by men. In 1824, explorer and businessman Charles C. Trowbridge interviewed Tenskwatawa, a prophet and leader and brother to Shawnee Chief Tecumseh. Tenskwatawa explained that the flute in ancient times had been used "by young men who were desirous of raising a war party. The leader, or he who wished to distinguish himself by setting afoot an expedition of this kind, would take his flute and retire a short distance from the village where he would begin to play. The young men around, at the sound of the music, assembled around him, and heard his declarations. If they chose to join him they pledged themselves upon the spot and joined in the song, but if they thought the project rash and inexpedient, they retired as they came. This instrument is now used by all young men, indiscriminately, and is not exclusively used by young men in love, though few in that situation fail to charm their mistresses with its sounds."

Observations by other explorers have survived as well, providing a picture of a rich, more diverse history of the flute than commonly promoted. During an expedition in 1528 in eastern Florida, Spanish explorer Alvar Nunez Cabeza de Vaca documented how "a chief approached, borne on the back of another Indian, and covered with a painted deer-skin. A great many people attended him, some walking in advance, playing on flutes of reed." A member of the Hernando de Soto Spanish 1539 Florida expedition wrote that "some Indians arrived to visit their lord, and every day they came out to the road, playing upon flutes, a token among them that they come in peace." In one account of an incident in what is now Alabama, the same writer observed "the Cacique came out to receive (de Soto)...and he was surrounded by many attendants playing upon flutes and singing."

Around 1540, Pedro de Castaneda recalled in his writings about the Pueblo Indians that "the people came out of the village with signs of joy to welcome Hernando de Alvardo and their captain, and brought with them into the town with drums and pipes something like flutes, of which they have a great many." Further, de Castaneda recorded that, during corn grinding, "a man sits at the door playing on a fife while they grind, moving the stones to the music and singing together." According to Antonio de Mendoza around the same time, "The Indians have their dances and songs, with some flutes which have holes on which to put the fingers. They make much noise. They sing in unison with those who play, and those who sing clap their hands in our fashion...five or six play together, and some of the flutes are better than others."

In 1602, Sebastian Vizcaino, in his account of experiences on Serros Island, the Mexican island now known as Cerros, wrote, "The Indians of the island came down to the beach where the water hole was made, with their bows and arrows, painted with vermillion, and playing flutes." English writer William Strachey wrote in 1612 about Indians in the Virginia colonies who "commonly bestow in reveling, dancing, and singing, and in their kind of music, and (they) have sundry instruments for the

same. They have a kind of cane, on which they pipe as on a recorder and are like the Greek pipes which they call bombices (*sic*), being hardly to be sounded without great strayning (*sic*) of the breath, upon which they observe certain rude tunes. Both their chief instruments are rattles made of small gourds...mingled with their voices sometimes twenty or thirty together makes such a terrible howling as would rather affright than give pleasure to any man."

Spanish soldier Pedro Fages, in his account of traveling through California in 1769, described how the flute was played by both men and women. Recalling a particular dance, he wrote, "...the women go to them well painted and dressed as has been described, carrying in both hands bundles of feathers of various colors. The men go entirely naked, but very much painted. Only two pairs from each sex are chosen to perform the dance, and two musicians, who play their flutes."

Music has never been the sole domain of men or women, but rather a communal experience, and the instruments used to make the music have been played by anyone who can play. From the start, music has accompanied joy, celebration, war, mourning, instruction, worship, and more—to be produced, shared, and experienced by everyone. To declare the flute as solely a man's instrument, used only in courting, is about as accurate as declaring the guitar an instrument only for men to seduce women. Yes, both have been used in courting, by both men and women, but so have many other instruments.

Still, the courting myth is a persistent and appealing tale, and it's easy for performers and pseudo historians to fall back on because it's so widely disseminated and popular. However, just as its history includes use by men and women in a variety of social experiences, the flute's origin stories include more tales than the love flute myth. In one story, a small bird fashions a flute to help a lost, mute child call to searchers. The piece that sits atop the flute is known as a *bird* to honor the generous bird that helped to save the child. In another tale, a chief and the village's elders become so bored with the music of their people, they journey to the home of the God of the Dew to ask for new music. The God of the Dew grants them their wish by fashioning and giving them four flutes on which they can make new and exciting music. In a particularly poignant tale, a chief's daughter dies tragically and is reincarnated as a loon, her soul trapped in the bird's body, unable to pass into the next world. Acting on the chief's prayers, the Great Spirit uses a lightning bolt to fashion a flute from a tree. The chief plays a prayer on the instrument, freeing the souls of his daughter and others from the loons so they can take their place in the next world.

Based on these and other myths and historical accounts, the flute was foremost a social instrument, used for the sheer joy of making music for personal and communal entertainment. Long before the arrival of Europeans, American Indian men and women who demonstrated a talent for playing the flute, usually at a young age, were encouraged and nurtured to continue their musical pursuit. Tribal members valued flute players, believing their musical ability was a gift from the Great Spirit or other deity. Gender was never an issue. The flute became a mainstay in various ceremonies defined by the particular tribe. The Hopi people, for example, not only valued the flute and flautists of both genders, they also integrated into the community a flute clan that developed the talents of flautists who would lead a flute-specific ceremony each autumn, designed to honor the gods and ensure good rains and crops. A girl and boy, side-by-side, both playing flutes, led the procession each year. Even today, despite dominance of the love flute myth, Native American flutes continue to be used in various ceremonies other than courting rituals, including weddings, ceremonies to honor various traditional gods, and official ceremonies such as appointments of new tribal leaders.

Structure

While it's known as the Native American *flute*, the name's misleading when referring to the modern version. Rather than a flute, the instrument is technically a whistle, resembling in design the European recorder. However, the ancient version was an end-blown flute similar to the Japanese *shakuhachi*, Chinese *xiao*, and Andean *quena*. Although the flute has long been a part of Native American life, no artifacts of the ancient version were known to have survived until, in 1931, Earl Morris, an archaeologist with the Carnegie Institute, began work in a cave, later named Broken Flute Cave, at the Prayer Rock district of northern Arizona, where he unearthed four remarkably preserved examples of the ancient end-blown version played by people of the Four Corners region, the area where Colorado, Utah, Arizona, and New Mexico meet.

The flutes are made of box elder wood, which has a soft inner pith that's easily removed to leave a hollow tube.

Remarkably preserved, the instruments date back at least 1,600 years to the period defined by pottery making, when people of the

Pictured here is one of the ancient flutes uncovered by Earl Morris. The distance between finger holes is considerable, making this an extremely difficult flute to play.

region lived in pithouses and the image known today as Kokopelli first appeared on the walls of many area caves. Of the flutes Morris found was buried with a male corpse, along with offerings of beads, baskets, and sandals, suggesting that the dead man was not a commoner, but perhaps a chief or priest. The flute had been placed atop the buried man's buckskin wrapping, one end tucked under his chin, the other between his thighs.

The Anasazi end-blown flute is a much simpler instrument to craft than the modern native flute, but it's a far more difficult instrument to play. The flautist's chin and lower mouth cover most of the blowing-end, while pursed lips channel air across the sharpened edge on the mouthpiece rim. A new player's first sound is likely to be nothing more than a rush of air. With luck, the player will produce a note within an hour or two, or it may take a week, but the sound, once achieved and perfected, proves hauntingly beautiful.

Flutes based on the artifact flutes' dimensions are physically challenging to play. About 30 inches long with finger holes spaced up to two inches apart, Anasazi flutes require a player with long arm reach and wide finger reach. Although the four artifact flutes are all about the same length, logic dictates that smaller versions were available because children were encouraged to play. Small hands and short arms simply cannot handle a flute with the dimensions of the artifacts. This book's crafting section for ancient flutes provides

the necessary percentages and formula for crafting sizes that best fit the needs of players. Although ancient flutes, as suggested by the four artifact flutes, appear to have been standardized in tuning, any existing tuning standards were lost when the jump was made from the end-blown to the modern two-chamber, whistle-type flute.

Prior to Morris's discovery of the Anasazi flute artifacts, the oldest surviving Native American flutes dated from the 1800s. Since woods used then for making the flutes decay rapidly, none had survived more than a few decades. A lucky conspiracy of local elements and grave preparation resulted in preservation of the four artifact flutes. Some flute aficionados speculate that the ancient version evolved into the modern version, in part, through tribes such as the Papago and Yuman who crafted two-chamber flutes using river cane. Early flute crafters found river cane, a bamboo species native to the Americas that can grow taller than thirty feet and have a diameter of 2-1/2 inches, perfectly suited for flute making. Crafters would remove all nodes but one from a particular piece of cane, then make a hole on either side of the remaining node. Some historians believe a player would direct air flow from the air chamber hole to the sound chamber hole with a thumb or finger. Eventually, a bird or fetish, with a shallow channel cut into either the fetish's underside or into the flute body between the air and sound holes, was utilized to direct air, leaving both hands to grasp the flute, allowing the maker to drill more finger holes and expand the instrument's scale.

Exactly when and how the flute transitioned from the Anasazi type to the two-chamber type remains a mystery. The early two-chamber native flute, unlike its predecessor, was an instrument unique to its individual crafter. A flute's length and placement of air, sound, and finger holes were dependent on the maker's physical measurements. (Directions for crafting a flute based on this technique are included in Chapter Eight.) It wasn't until the mid-twentieth century that dimensions and tuning were standardized.

Reviving Interest

As Europeans vanquished resistance and relegated native families to reservations, many of the children were taken from their families and placed in Indian boarding schools, established by Christian missionaries with governmental blessing. Native children were forbidden to wear traditional clothing, speak their cultural languages, go by their tribal names, or discuss their own peoples' history, which had been preserved by an oral accounting from generation to generation. Instead, they were immersed in European studies and culture. With heritage and history previously preserved through stories told from generation to generation, aspects of native culture began to vanish.

The erosion of native life, culture, and pride resulted in declining interest in the flute, and its use and prevalence faded through the late 1800s and into the 1900s. Traditions were lost, history forgotten or never learned, and what had once been native culture became

nothing more than European propaganda. By the early 1900s, the flute had become a novelty racing toward complete obscurity. Had it not been for a surgeon from Oklahoma City whose interest bordered obsession, the Native American flute may have become just another mysterious artifact, collecting dust in museums.

By the 1950s, Dr. Richard Payne had become an avid collector, player, and craftsman of vintage Native American flutes, his interest in the instrument kindled before World War II. As he amassed the collection of flutes and whistles common to tribes throughout the Americas, he became a walking encyclopedia on the instrument, gathering and compiling information through extensive visits with players who had kept traditional music alive.

One key aspect of the flutes Payne collected was the lack of standardized construction. Each flute was a solo instrument, tuned to itself and to no standard scale. Payne began to experiment with the traditional instrument's design with the goal of developing a flute versatile enough to play both native melodies and contemporary melodies, providing to modern music a unique sound that could be incorporated with other instruments.

Experimenting with various softwoods, including cedar, Payne eventually standardized the instrument to the pentatonic scale, an approximate scale to the traditional method of crafting. With a standard scale in place, the native flute could now be used to play standard tunes with accompanying instruments while retaining the ability to render traditional Native American tunes as a solo instrument. Payne's *The Native American Plains Flute*, an independently published book that can be found through some online dealers, details the collector's research, providing detailed diagrams of flutes he studied as he developed his theory of how the Native American flute evolved from ancient end-blown flutes into the modern two-chamber version.

Thanks to Payne and the popular artists who followed— Coyote Oldman, Mary Youngblood, R. Carlos Nakai, and many others—awareness of the Native American flute surged and continues to grow. Musicians have expanded the instrument's reach into jazz, rock, world, and other music genres, providing listeners and players alike with a soulful experience enriched by a broadening knowledge of the flute's history and development. For more detailed exploration of the mythology and history of the flute, please refer to *The Native American Flute: Myth, History, Craft.*

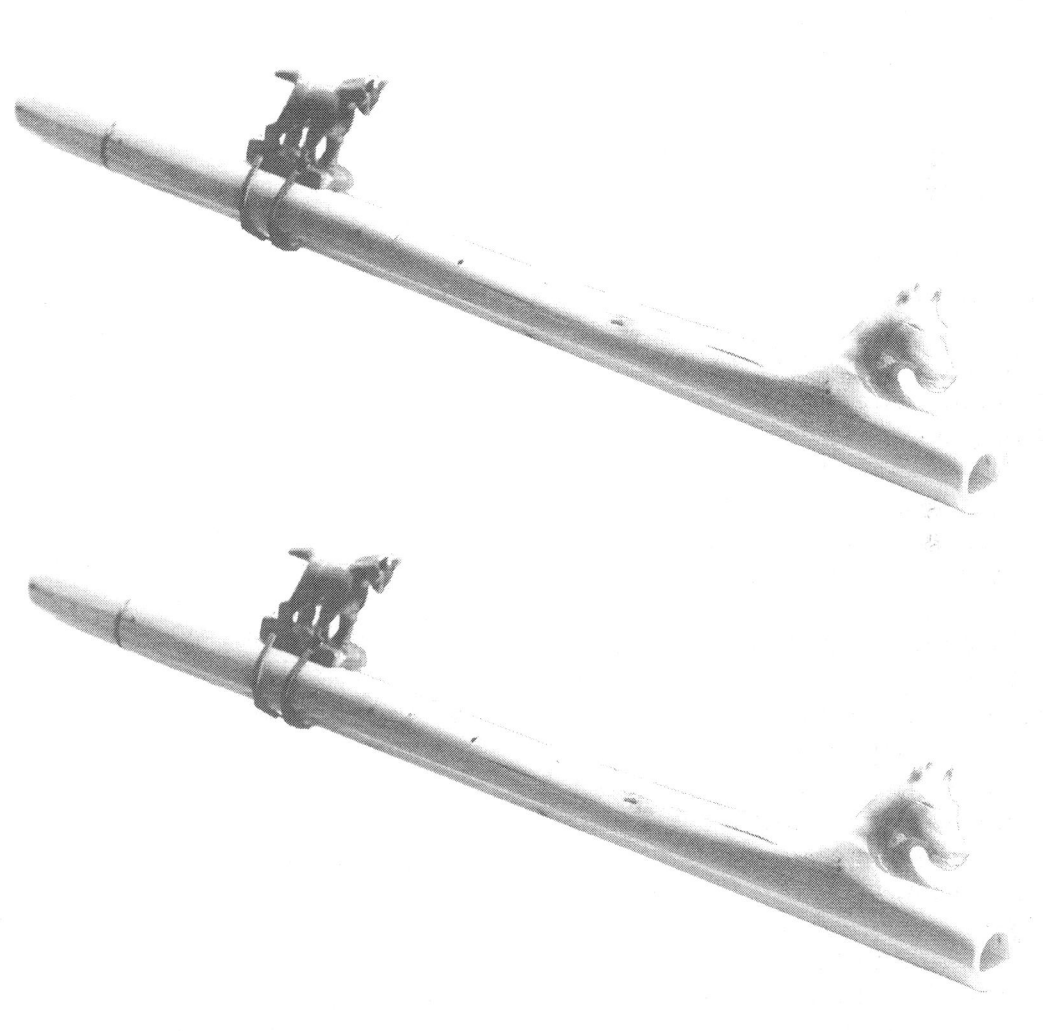

Chapter Two

Flute Material

The flute, in its various forms worldwide, is the oldest indigenous musical instrument, second only to the drum. The earliest known flutes date back at least 35,000 years, the oldest artifact thus far uncovered in southwestern Germany, made of a hollow, 8-1/2-inch bird bone, with five finger holes. A second flute, made from a mammoth's tusk, measuring a little more than seven inches with three finger holes, was also uncovered in Germany and dates back some 30,000 years to the European Ice Age.

These flutes, while the oldest surviving artifact flutes, most likely do not represent the earliest flutes crafted. They survive because they're made from a highly durable and long-lasting material, bone. Flutes pre-dating, during, and after these flutes were most likely crafted from materials that decayed more easily, materials such as

wood and bamboo. Bamboo and wooden flutes are mentioned in the literature of various cultures, from Chinese to Egyptian, dating back to 1550 B.C.E., but the oldest surviving artifact flutes from most cultures are, like those discovered in Germany, made from bone. The four Anasazi flutes discovered in Arizona are an anomaly.

Munich-born Theobald Boehm, a jeweler and goldsmith, redesigned the traditional side-blown flute in 1832 to standardize it for inclusion in orchestral work, crafting the new version from metal instead of wood. Today's conventional side-blown flutes still conform to Boehm's design. Folk flutes, on the other hand, continue to be crafted primarily from the same materials as they were in the beginning. As already mentioned, few examples of ancient flutes of the Americas have survived. Besides the four Anasazi flutes uncovered by Earl

Morris at Broken Flute Cave, other indigenous American flute artifacts dating from or before that era are made of clay, products fashioned primarily by Mesoamerican peoples, including the Mayan and Aztec cultures. Today's multi-barrel drone version of the Native American flute may have evolved from the region around Colima, sometime between 300 to 150 B.C.E. Researchers believe double flutes were used primarily to enhance religious rituals.

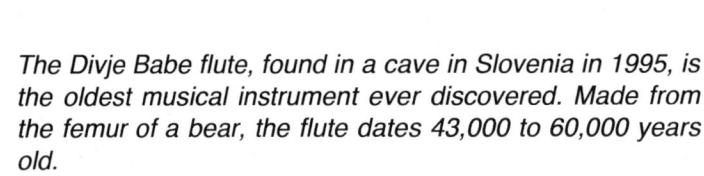

The Divje Babe flute, found in a cave in Slovenia in 1995, is the oldest musical instrument ever discovered. Made from the femur of a bear, the flute dates 43,000 to 60,000 years old.

Today, most crafters of the Native American flute use woods considered traditional in the craft. Others craft flutes from clay, mimicking the Mesoamerican tradition, some utilizing the ceramic fire method while others achieve similar results with no-fire clays designed to air-dry. Each crafter has an opinion on sound quality, claiming that this or that material is superior to others. Early crafters were probably not as concerned with sound quality as they were with a material's workability for shaping into a playable instrument. Softwoods were chosen for their ease in hollowing. Bamboo was and remains a natural for flute-making. And clay was a good choice for Mesoamericans because they were already masters in the art of ceramics.

In our anything's-available world of diminishing and threatened resources, we can pick and choose and argue over the plusses and minuses of materials that are both traditional and non-traditional in the crafting of flutes. The following sections in this chapter explore the sound qualities of several materials, but choice comes down to what pleases ears of the crafter and player. Some swear by the sound qualities of one material over another. Others insist that material—bamboo, wood, clay, PVC—doesn't matter as much as the quality of craftsmanship. Whatever material you choose for crafting flutes, choose for personal preference. And if it's bamboo or wood, make sure it is sustainably sourced.

Bamboo

If any material is best suited for crafting flutes and whistles, bamboo is the one. That's why bamboo is the dominant choice for flutes in so many cultures around the world, from the Japanese *shakuhachi* to the Andean *quena* to the Chinese *xiao* to the Indian *bansuri* and more.

In the Americas, especially in what is now the southeastern region of the United States, early bamboo flutes were crafted from what's known as river cane, a *monopodial leptomorphic* bamboo—the fancy way of saying it spreads laterally by underground rhizomes and can continue indefinitely under favorable conditions. River cane thrives in moist, neutral to acidic soils. Fully grown, it can top heights of thirty feet and reach diameters of three inches or more. Depending on age and specific variety, the culms, those sections between nodes, are often up to two feet long, lending themselves perfectly to flute-making. Makers and players alike cite bamboo's *warm* and *clean* sound. For many, its structure and sound quality make it the *only* choice for crafting flutes, whether side-blown, end-blown, or two chamber.

Bamboo has a major drawback, however—a propensity to split. Especially in dry conditions and climates that experience extreme fluctuations in humidity, splitting is bamboo's most common liability. Even so, several steps can be taken to deter splitting and extend the life of a bamboo instrument. First, store the instrument in a humidified case. Second, finish it with lacquer to seal the material and deter harmful effects of humidity fluctuation. Third, bind the flute with ties that reinforce its natural strength. Even when these measures are taken, however, the fragility of bamboo, despite its suitability to flute-making, makes it less desirable to some crafters and players.

Wood

Instrument crafters, primarily those of stringed instruments, believe the best wood is aged wood—not only aged, but aged in water, such as a lake or river. Such prized aged wood in condition good enough for making instruments comes at a premium price. Since the wood's age has less detectable effect on the sound quality of a native flute than the quality of a stringed instrument, most native flute crafters bypass suppliers of prime aged wood and, instead, rely on local, mail order, and online suppliers for wood that's more readily affordable. Others cut their own wood, which is fine if it's taken from a sustainable source or from naturally-downed trees and limbs. Cutting fresh wood from a non-sustainable environment simply to craft flutes is irresponsible and in direct conflict with what the Native American flute has come to symbolize in the popular psyche, an instrument with spiritual implications.

When selecting wood for a flute, consider durability, tonal quality, and visual appeal. Softwoods, such as cedar and pine, were the choice for early flutes strictly because they were soft and could be easily shaped with simple tools. Today, crafters aren't limited to softwoods. Access to specialized woodworking tools makes wood choice one of specific taste and desire, from softwoods like pine, cedar, and poplar to dense, hardwoods like oak, walnut, and maple.

Whether soft or hard, wood's major advantage over bamboo is durability and resistance to breakage and splitting. Wood adapts more readily to its environment, but extreme fluctuations in humidity can have dire effects, including splitting if humidity remains extremely low for long periods. However, simple and easy measures, which will be discussed later, can prevent humidity-related damage to flutes.

Wood density affects the sound quality of instruments, making some woods better suited than others for specific types of instruments. With instruments such as guitars or xylophones, a wood's properties affect volume, quality, and color of sound through vibration. Soundboards for instruments such as xylophones are crafted from high-density wood. For wind instruments such as native flutes, woods of different densities are regularly used. While conventional side-blown flutes are made primarily from dense woods, providing stability of material and sound even when exposed to high levels of moisture that result from playing, Native American flutes have been traditionally crafted from softwoods, which remain the standard choice of material for modern native flutes.

The type of material used to craft a flute affects sound through vibrational damping (gradual reduction of vibration) due to air friction along tube walls and turbulence in the vibrating air at the edges, which also affects tonal quality. Damping is lower in tubes with a smooth finish, suggesting that high density and fine-grained woods are best suited for clear, sustained tones. Softwoods tend to deliver a more mellow, perhaps *muddier*, tone than hardwoods. However, finishes such as lacquer can be used on softwoods to smooth air flow and produce a cleaner sound similar to that of hardwood flutes.

In general, softwoods, such as pine and cedar, are easy to work with and provide a soulful, mellow sound. On the other hand, flutes made of hardwoods, such as boxwood, an extremely dense wood, are more difficult to craft, but are sturdier, less susceptible to damage, and produce a clear, more sustained tone. Preferred hardwoods for flute-making include boxwood, ebony, African blackwood, rosewood, and maple, all aesthetically beautiful. Softwoods well-suited for crafting include aromatic red cedar (the most popular wood for crafting native flutes), pine, and poplar. Although poplar is technically a hardwood as defined by species, it is softer than pine and is readily and affordably available.

Although wood choice isn't as critical in flute-making as it is in crafting stringed instruments, it still affects overall sound quality, however small or large. What it comes down to is the crafter's or player's preference. Today's ready access to power tools makes any choice of wood for crafting flutes a reasonable choice.

When crafting with wood, be aware that dust from cutting and sanding poses respiratory health risks. Always wear a good quality respiratory dust mask or respirator.

PVC

Polyvinyl chloride (PVC) pipe is a popular and inexpensive choice for crafting flutes, despite the debate over the material's possible health risks. Developed in the early 1900s, polyvinyl chloride was first used in commercial applications as wiring insulation. Today, it's become the third most utilized plastic in the world, offering an inexpensive, durable material suited for numerous purposes. PVC is used mostly in construction applications, from insulation and window frames to flooring and shower curtains and more. PVC plumbing pipes are a popular first choice for makers of all types of flutes, providing an inexpensive alternative to wood and bamboo for both crafter and musician. However, concern exists over health risks and environmental dangers associated with PVC and its components.

PVC, when burned, releases extremely dangerous gases, including hydrogen chloride, a corrosive and toxic gas that can burn skin and cause permanent and severe respiratory damage. Burning also releases dioxin, the most dangerous of manmade carcinogens. In fact, PVC is the largest contributor to dioxin pollution. The material's essential component, vinyl chloride, is a carcinogen and potentially explosive when released from PVC. According to the Environmental Protection Agency, it can enter drinking water in contact with PVC pipes. Breathing PVC dust can result in both acute and long-term respiratory and other health issues. Therefore, when working with PVC, exercise high caution. Wear protective gear such as a dust mask or ventilator, and never burn the material.

Clay

Clay, along with wood and bamboo, is the material native flute crafters have used for millennia. Mesoamericans commonly crafted flutes with clay. Today's clays are readily available in two types, those that require firing, and those that can be air-dried, offering an exciting alternative to wooden and plastic flutes. Clay's obvious advantage is its ability to be molded into a flute that is artistically unique to the crafter, limited only by the crafter's imagination. Its primary disadvantages are workability and durability.

A person attempting to craft a flute with clay should have prior experience in ceramic work since the material will prove a challenge in every stage of flute creation. Clay, even after firing or drying, is extremely susceptible to breakage and chipping. If it's an air-dried flute, it should be coated with a moisture resistant finish such as lacquer. Otherwise, conventional clay molds can quickly deteriorate and crumble from the moisture of the player's breath.

Clay also poses possible health risks. All clays contain crystalline silica, from trace amounts to as much as 50 percent. Respiratory exposure to crystalline silica can scar lung tissue and decrease breathing capacity. Since particulate matter can remain in the air for hours, always wear a mask when working with clay, especially if sanding dry clay. Decrease risk to exposure by working with premixed, wet clay. Work in an area that has good ventilation, utilize a respiratory filter, and wear vinyl-type aprons rather than cloth aprons. Follow all manufacturer instructions and warnings to minimize risks to health.

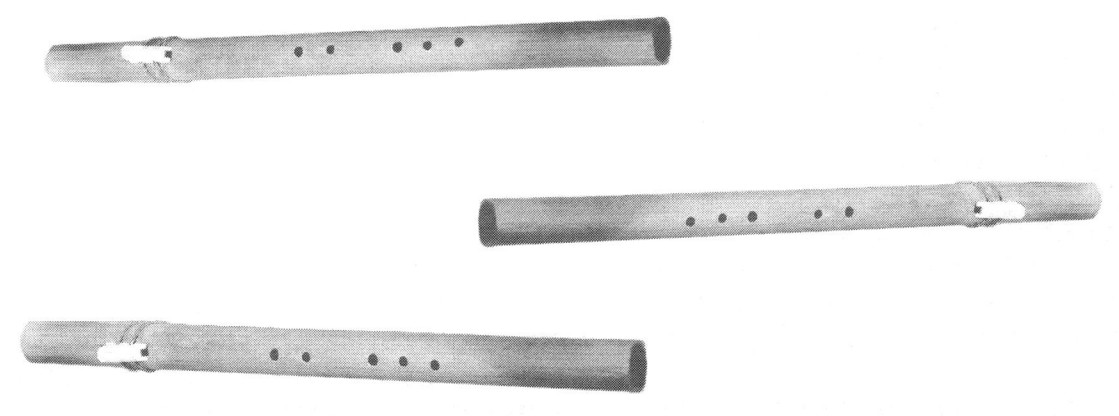

Chapter Three

Finishes

Whether bamboo or wood, or even PVC, the material used to craft a Native American flute will probably require a finish as either protectant or decoration. A final protective finish should be applied to all flutes crafted of wood and bamboo, and several types of finish are available. The number of products appropriate for PVC and clay finishes is more limited than the number available for wood. And while PVC requires no finish at all, clay, especially air-dried clay, even more than wood or bamboo, requires application of a finish to both exterior and interior to prevent the clay from eventually disintegrating from moisture.

Standard finishes for wood and bamboo include wax, lacquer, a variety of oils, varnish, shellac, and polyurethane. Finishes fall into two basic categories: evaporative finishes that dry to a hard coating as solvents evaporate, and reactive finishes that cure by reacting to the air outside the container or to a chemical added before application. Evaporative finishes, such as lacquer and shellac, will redissolve long after they've been applied and dried if subjected to solvents originally used for thinning. Reactive finishes, such as tung oil or linseed oil, will not redissolve in solvents originally used to thin them, but reactive finishes must be reapplied regularly to protect the wood adequately.

In choosing a finish, consider first the material from which the flute is crafted. For wood and bamboo, all of the above finishes are possibilities. For clay, the flutes should be glazed or, if air-dried, sealed with a moisture repelling finish such as waterproof sealant, acrylic paint, waterproof lacquer, or varnish. If the flute is PVC or other plastic, then the only finish needed is decorative, such as paint or colored lacquer.

Choice of finish is affected directly by type of appearance desired—glossy, satin, painted—the finish's enhancing and darkening factors, and the maintenance the finish requires after application. For a natural appearance, the usual choice is oil, although a natural, non-stained look can be accomplished with most finishes, including varnish, lacquer, and shellac. Oil, oil-based varnishes, and solvent-based shellac and lacquer darken wood somewhat. However, some varnishes and shellacs will darken wood considerably more than desired. Some finishes will yellow in time, an effect that's more noticeable on lighter woods. It's always best to test a finish's effect on a piece of scrap wood before applying it to the flute.

Solvent-based finishes, such as lacquer and varnish, are extremely flammable and harmful to both health and environment in application form. The good news is that, after the solvents have evaporated and the finishes have fully cured, all solvent-based finishes are nontoxic. During the drying process, however, the finishes release volatile organic compounds (VOC) that can cause eye and skin irritation, breathing problems, headaches, nausea, muscle weakness, and, in extreme circumstances, damage to the kidneys and liver. Working in a well-ventilated area, preferably outdoors, is recommended. Even outside, though, VOCs combine with other pollutants to exacerbate already existing problems with standard air quality.

Various wood finishes can also contain other toxic ingredients, including dioxane and acetaldehyde (both suspected carcinogens), toluene, n-methyl pyrrolidinone, and xylene. Lead, a toxic metal, was once used in some oil and resin varnishes as a metallic drier, but it has been replaced with other metals that include cobalt and zinc. However, even these replacement metals cause problems because of toxicity and persistence in the environment. As a result of governmental environmental regulations, ozone-depleting compounds have been phased out of most products, but phthalates that are still used in plasticizers and can affect a person's hormonal system.

Due to these potentially harmful ingredients, regulations, such as the Clean Air Act, and consumer desire for safer products, manufacturers have introduced products with lower VOCs. To achieve lower VOCs, newer finishes do not always penetrate the wood as well as higher VOC finishes. Finishes designed specifically for lower VOCs use water as the thinning agent and offer minimal solvent fumes and easy cleanup. They raise the wood's grain, however, and are not as resistant to water, heat, and solvents as conventional finishes. To ensure full protection, several coats of the lower VOC finishes may be required.

Wax

Wax can be applied over another finish or used as a stand-alone finish. Bees' wax, carnauba wax, and petroleum-based synthetic waxes are readily available in both liquid and paste forms. Wax should be applied with a dry cloth in several coats, the number depending on the level of shine and protection desired. Follow manufacturer recommendations for best results. Although it offers moderate protection against moisture, wax provides little to no protection against abrasive damage such as scratches. Wax must be reapplied periodically since its protection and appearance lessen with age.

Oil

Finishing oils, such as tung and linseed oil, are readily available and a favorite among woodworkers of all stripes, including flute makers. Tung oil and linseed oil are finishes that penetrate the wood's fibers to harden and provide moderate protection to the wood from moisture and environmental damage. Oils are applied easily with an oil-dampened cloth. Excess oil should be wiped from the wood before the project's allowed to dry.

Superficial damage to the flute's surface, such as a scratch or ding, is easily fixed by light sanding and reapplication of oil. However, superficial damage is common because, like wax, oil does not provide hard-coat protection. And though it's used to deter moisture damage, water can still penetrate and harm the wood. Other liquids can also penetrate an oil finish to stain the wood. Stains can prove far more difficult to remove than scratches.

Like wax, oil finishes require reapplication to maintain an adequate level of protection and appearance. The rate of reapplication will vary from player to player and location to location. The flute will have a soft, satin luster after application. As the oil dries and is rubbed off by player use, the wood will lose its patina and appear dry, indicating the need for oil reapplication.

Some crafters and players prefer to skip all conventional finishing oils in preference of products less common in woodworking such as olive oil. Such oils, however, provide minimal protection from moisture and must be reapplied often.

Varnish

Varnish finish is comprised of both natural and synthetic resins, such as phenolic and alkyd, in an oil-based solvent, such as tung oil or linseed oil, along with drying oils such as soybean. Although it cures in the same way as oil finishes, varnish results in a more durable and protective finish with higher resistance to moisture, chemicals, and heat than its oil counterparts. Although standard varnish is applied with a brush, varnish designed specifically for application with a rag is also available.

Shellac

Shellac is one of the most common hard finishes used by flute makers. Made by dissolving a natural resin secreted by the southeast Asian Lac beetle in denatured alcohol, shellac is available in both premixed and user-mix forms. It provides a finish that penetrates the fibers of the wood to enhance the wood's color and create a hard, damage-resistant surface. Premixed shellac comes in amber and clear. Numerous colors are available in the flake, user-mix version.

Shellac's drawbacks include the tendency to tint light-colored wood slightly yellow. A softer finish than varnish or lacquer, it is more susceptible to dents and scratches and may even dissolve into a sticky state under extremely hot, humid conditions.

Polyurethane

Polyurethane is a plastic finish that can be either oil or water based, providing a hard, transparent, glossy finish to wood. Although most woodworkers prefer lacquers to polyurethane, polyurethane produces the hardest, most durable finish used in woodworking and is a favorite for finishing wood flooring. It's applied by brush and is slow to cure, requiring a minimum 24-hour drying time between coats.

Polyurethane is highly flammable during the application process and requires a well-ventilated area since its vapors pose health risks.

Lacquer

Lacquer, like polyurethane, requires good ventilation and care during application due to its extreme combustibility and risk to health. Lacquer is a resin-based solution that dries into a hard, transparent coating when exposed to air. Subsequent coats can be applied relatively quickly since each new coat "melts" into the previous coat, hardening rapidly to provide a durable and attractive finish. Although adequate drying between coats is quick, complete curing can take several weeks, depending on the number of coats applied and environmental conditions.

Besides being more resistant to stains and abrasion than varnish, lacquer is also more resistant to moisture, making it an excellent choice to counter potential moisture problems caused by the player's breath, acting as a strong deterrent to the absorption of moisture that collects in the flute's chambers.

Woodworkers prefer lacquer for numerous reasons, including its ability to enhance the richness of the wood while providing strong protection. Its biggest drawback is a tendency to yellow with time, most evident on light colored woods.

Water-Based Finishes

Commercially available water-based finishes are much like their conventional counterparts in content, containing components such as urethane and acrylic, but with water replacing most flammable and polluting ingredients used in conventional finishes. Resins are chemically modified to combine with water. Water-based finishes are not, in general, as strong as their conventional oil-based counterparts, but they offer a more environmentally friendly choice for finishing a flute.

My Preference

I prefer to apply an initial coat of linseed or tung oil to flutes of wood and bamboo. After the oil dries, I complete the finish with several coats of clear lacquer. The oil enhances the color of the wood, defining the grain. The lacquer, which further enhances the wood's appearance, provides a strong, protective coat. I've chosen this finishing process to protect against potential damage from humidity fluctuation.

One of my early bamboo flutes was a favorite, one I played regularly. But I had used only linseed oil as its finish. At the time, I lived in North Alabama where humidity was usually above sixty percent, making humidification of instruments a low priority or need. One night during a period of unusually low humidity, I had been playing only a few minutes when the bamboo split the entire length of the flute. The inside was quite damp from moisture that had condensed from my breath. The bamboo couldn't absorb and expand rapidly enough, causing it to split. Since then, I have finished all bamboo flutes and most wooden flutes with lacquer. So far, I've enjoyed extremely positive results.

Most PVC flutes I leave unfinished, but some I finish with black lacquer to make them more aesthetically appealing.

For wooden flutes, I use either oil or lacquer, depending on the specific flute and whether I want a glossy finish or a satin finish. I prefer satin finishes in general, and so the majority of wood flutes are finished exclusively with linseed or tung oil. Of course, re-oiling is required every few months, but it's only a minor inconvenience to maintain and protect an instrument I enjoy playing.

I have finished only one flute with wax. In my opinion, wax provides too little protection for the initial application and subsequent maintenance it requires.

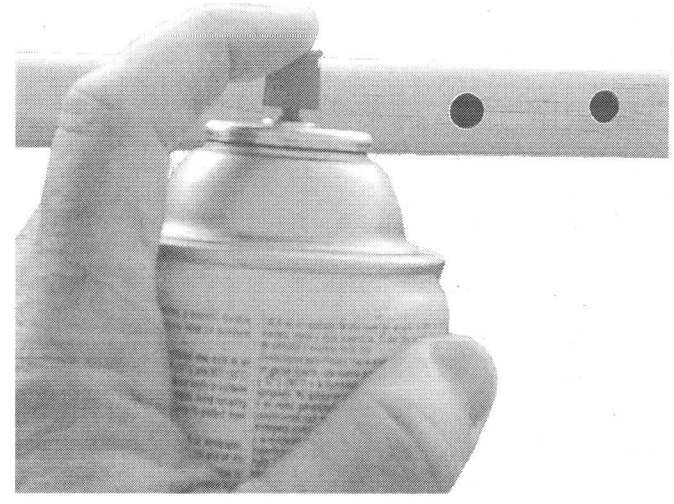

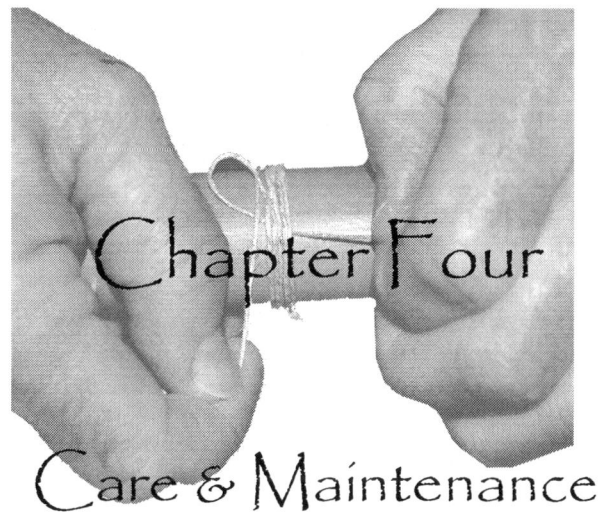

Chapter Four
Care & Maintenance

Once you've crafted an instrument that's both aesthetically and technically satisfying, you'll want to keep it in the best condition possible. With basic care, you can prolong the life of your instrument by years, decades, even lifetimes.

PVC and Clay Flutes

A flute crafted from PVC requires very little maintenance beyond an occasional wash if it isn't painted. If painted, simply wipe the exterior and chamber interiors occasionally, exercising caution to prevent scuffs and scratches.

If you've crafted a clay flute, you probably have prior experience working with clay and caring for the end products. In general, other than handling the instrument carefully to prevent breakage, little maintenance is required for a clay flute that has been properly fired or air-dried, sealed, and finished to pre-vent damage from moisture. After playing, clean the instrument with a soft cloth to maintain an unobstructed surface and dry moisture condensation from the barrel interior and under the fetish, moisture that could otherwise form residue that accumulates over time, degrading sound production.

Wood and Bamboo Flutes

Variations in humidity and temperature are a wood or bamboo flute's worst enemy. Cracks and splits in wooden and bamboo flutes are usually the result of extreme variation in temperature or humidity or due to extended dry periods that result in wood fibers shrinking and pulling apart. Changes in heat and humidity cause the wood to shrink and expand. If the flute changes too quickly, it can, and probably will, split, especially if it's bamboo. Even the best made flutes from topline woods are susceptible.

High humidity affects the sound of an instrument by causing the wood to swell. A flute played for an extended period is subject to this effect as moisture from the player's breath gathers under the fetish, increasingly diminishing sound quality until air flow may cease completely. On a properly sealed and finished flute, cleaning the buildup away with a cloth usually solves the problem. Such moisture condensation more profoundly affects a flute that isn't properly finished. Both the flute's wood and wooden fetish may swell to the point the flute becomes unplayable even when wiped dry, the swelling effectively blocking the channel. Not until the wood has dried will the flute become playable again. To deter swelling from breath condensation, finish the wood with a moisture resistant product and wipe the flute's barrel, channel, and bird underside with a clean cloth during and immediately after a playing session. If the slow air chamber is inaccessible except through the mouthpiece hole, store the flute vertically with the mouthpiece downward to drain excess moisture.

Protective Case

While structural damage is less likely in high humidity environments, low humidity environments can damage, even destroy, a flute quickly, especially one made of bamboo. The fibers in wood and bamboo do not lose or gain moisture evenly. Rapid uneven loss of moisture will cause fibers to pull away from one another, resulting in splits and cracks.

Low humidity is a constant concern in areas such as the southwestern United States. But residents in all climates should take precautions to prevent damage from fluctuations in humidity, especially in winter. The best way to protect against humidity-related damage is to store the flute in a case that provides protection from environmental variations. Numerous types of cases are available from various online sellers, with soft carry bags one of the most popular. Cloth carry bags, however, provide minimal protection against variations in humidity. Hard plastic cases are also available, many equipped with a cloth exterior and shoulder strap for easy portability. Such cases provide good, protective storage, but they can be quite expensive. A simple, inexpensive, alternative case can be easily crafted without tools. All that's needed is a PVC tube, two PVC end caps, and foam padding. Most local hardware stores carry end caps and precut PVC pipes in various diameters and lengths, including economically priced pipes of eight feet and longer that can yield several cases for less cost than a pre-cut pipe. For padding, inexpensive foam mattress toppers are available from most department and discount stores.

Materials

- PVC pipe at least one inch longer and twice the diameter of the flute or group of flutes you want to protect.
- two PVC end caps
- foam rubber, available in different thicknesses as mattress toppers

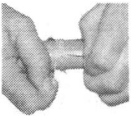

Craft the Case

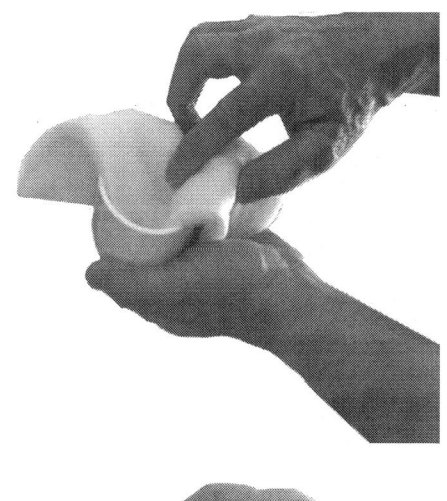

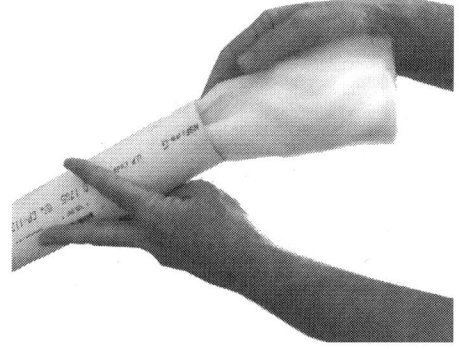

1. Cut a circle of foam to fill each end cap.

2. Cut a length of foam to line the inside of the PVC pipe. If the pipe is going to be used for multiple flutes, or for added protection of a single flute, cut a length of foam in which to wrap the individual flute.

Humidity fluctuations are especially worrisome in winter when humidity is normally low but can fluctuate drastically from day to day. Store flutes away from heating sources and near the floor since air is cooler with a slightly higher humidity at lower levels. Maintain interior temperatures at 68° to 70° Fahrenheit. Lower interior temperatures are economically and ecologically wise and maintain a higher humidity than excessively warm temperatures.

Case Humidifier

During extended periods of low humidity, place a humidifier in the instrument case. Of course, expensive case humidifiers are available, but all that's needed for adequate case humidification is a small plastic container and a sponge, available in a range of sizes from most department and grocery stores.

1. Punch several 1/8-inch holes in the top of the plastic container.

2. Cut the sponge into squares to fill the container.

3. Soak the sponge with water and squeeze out the excess.

4. Place the sponge in the container and snap on the cover.

5. Place the container in the tube with the instrument.

6. Check the humidifier regularly, depending on local humidity levels.

7. Dampen the sponge as needed.

Binding

Although a case equipped with a humidifier will battle effects of low humidity, bamboo may need extra protection afforded by binding to deter splits and cracks from developing. Use a strong twine or string to bind the flute between the mouthpiece and fetish, sound hole and sixth finger hole, and foot and first finger hole, as long as binding in these locations doesn't deter playing. Refer to the binding illustration and following photographs. If you wrap only one section, choose the mouthpiece end since most splits result along the slow air chamber due to rapid humidity change caused by breath moisture during playing.

Choose the binding string for strength. Although thin string may be preferable for appearance, thick string will prove easier to use. Thinner string will afford more wrapping ability within a given space. Before binding the flute, practice with a piece of scrap wood, dowel, or PVC. Wear eye protection to prevent damage from string recoil in case of breakage.

1. Unroll two feet of string from the roll.

2. Tie one end of the string to a dowel to hold on the floor with your feet.

3. At the binding point on the flute, form and tape to the barrel a loop two to three inches in size, depending on the width of the planned wrap.

4. Keeping the string taut, wrap it around the barrel by rolling the flute. When finished wrapping, cut the string between the flute and source.

5. Thread the cut end through the loop, and remove the tape.

6. Pull the loop by its end under the binding to the center.

7. Snip the string ends close to the wrap. The binding's tension holds the knot secure.

8. Apply a finish to the binding, such as slow-cure epoxy, pol-

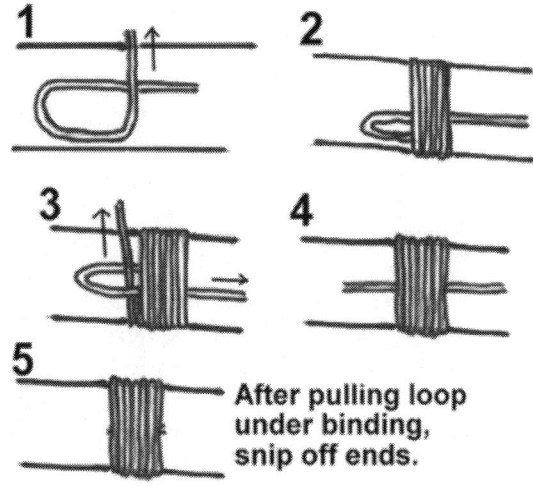

After pulling loop under binding, snip off ends.

yurethane, or Super Glue, to deter loosening. Apply the finish *only* to the string. The binding will loosen over time, requiring rebinding, but it's a simple procedure that can extend the life of a bamboo flute for many years.

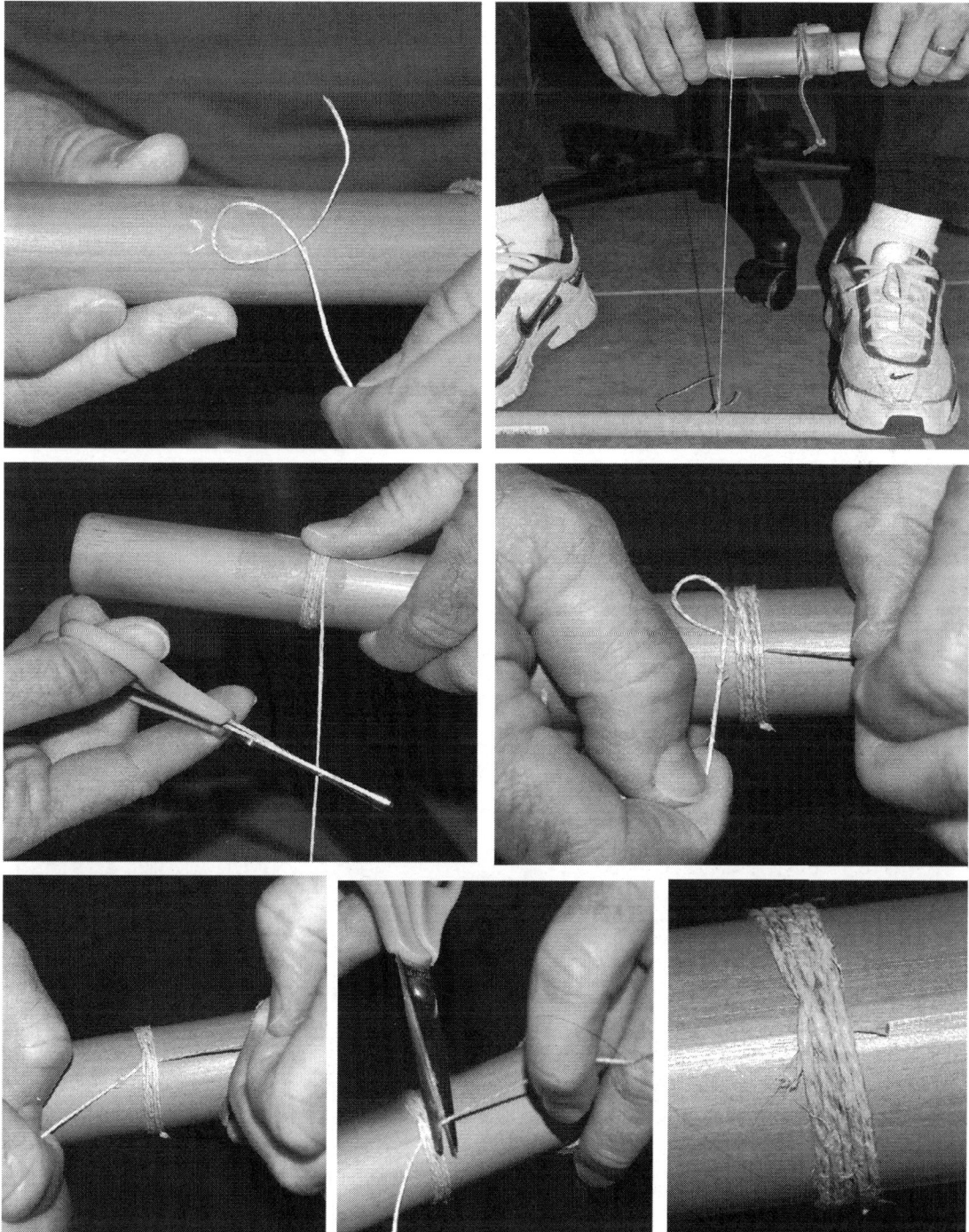

Crack & Split Repair

At some point, a bamboo flute will probably develop a split in line with the grain. A split in bamboo can result from abuse, dropping the flute onto a hard surface, or extreme moisture variation, causing the bamboo fibers to contract too rapidly. If it doesn't go completely through the bamboo from exterior to interior, a crack caused by low humidity can sometimes be closed by wrapping the affected area with a damp cloth for several hours to several days, replacing moisture the bamboo has lost to the environment. After the crack closes, bind the bamboo using the method previously described.

If the crack goes completely through the bamboo wall, it can be closed and sealed in many cases by using one of several kinds of glue, based on preference. I prefer wood glue.

1. Fill the crack with glue and apply pressure evenly around the bamboo, closing the crack, forcing out excess glue.

2. Carefully bind or clamp the flute to keep the crack closed.

3. Allow the glue to dry at least 24 hours before releasing the binding or clamp.

4. After the glue has dried, bind the flute with twine as previously described.

General Flute Care

1. If the flute is not lacquered, oil it at least quarterly, more often if played regularly or kept in a dry climate. Use walnut oil, tung oil, linseed oil, mineral oil, or other natural nut oil.

2. Do not subject the flute to sudden or extreme changes in temperature and humidity. For example, do not take a flute from an air-conditioned house into daytime heat. Leave the flute in its case to allow it to adjust gradually to temperature changes.

3. Do not place the flute near a heating or cooling source.

4. Do not leave the flute in a car on a hot or cold day. Think of it as a pet or child.

5. Do not leave the flute in direct sunlight.

6. Do not store a flute on a car's dashboard, subjecting it to direct sunlight.

7. Do not play bamboo flutes in cold surroundings, especially bamboo flutes that are not properly bound and finished with a moisture resistant product. The player's warm, moist breath can rapidly expand the interior while the outer surface remains cold and resistant to expansion. The result can be a split fatal to the instrument.

8. Wipe dry any condensation formed on the flute's interior

and exterior while playing. If the air chamber is inaccessible, store the flute vertically with the mouthpiece down.

9. Do not knock or drop the flute against a hard surface.

10. Bind both bamboo and wooden flutes for enhanced durability.

11. Never store the flute in a precarious location, such as a bookshelf, where it can be easily knocked off, or on the floor where it might be stepped on.

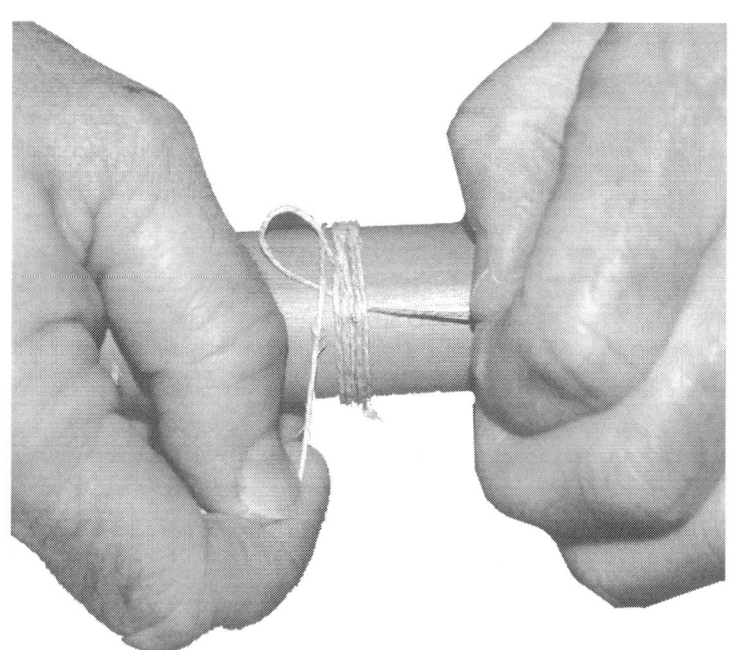

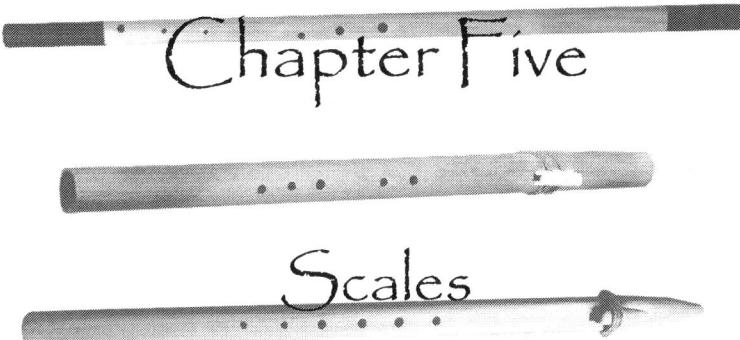

Chapter Five

Scales

Native American flutes made by different crafters vary in more ways than appearance. The standard pentatonic scale that plays perfectly on one crafter's flute may not play the same on another crafter's flute. The reason is usually due to fingerings. Fingerings typical to most native flutes don't always play exactly the same notes on *all* native flutes. Why? The native flute is a folk instrument, crafted most often by hand, which lends itself to both minor and major variations, especially when the flutes are products of different crafters. In fact, variations are common in flutes made by the *same* crafter. Even so, the basic scale—the *do, re, me, fa, so, la, te, do*—will, in most cases, be fingered the same or close to the same on most native flutes. Variations occur primarily in the extended scale. Although the following discussion covers the usual extended scale fingerings, compensation and alternate fingerings may be required for different flutes to achieve specific notes.

That doesn't make any particular flute better or worse than another. It makes it unique.

Most modern Native American flutes utilize the pentatonic scale. The note produced by the first finger hole is 1.5 steps higher than the fundamental note, and each successive finger hole note is one step higher than the preceding hole's note. For example, F# 6-hole and 5-hole flutes would have the following fundamental/root and finger hole notes:

6-hole Flute

- F#: fundamental note
- A: hole 1
- B: hole 2
- C#: hole 3
- D#/Eb: hole 4
- F: hole 5
- G: hole 6

5-hole Flute

- ➤ F#: fundamental note
- ➤ A: hole 1
- ➤ B: hole 2
- ➤ C#: hole 3
- ➤ E: hole 4
- ➤ F#: hole 5

Some crafters use alternate scales for their flutes, but this book explores only the standard pentatonic scale used to craft the majority of modern Native American flutes. However, the pentatonic scale is not applicable if the traditional, pre-standardized method of flute crafting is utilized. Although the notes will come close to the pentatonic scale, each flute will be unique, and its degree of variation from the standard scale will depend on the crafter's physical attributions. (Please refer to crafting the traditional native flute section in Chapter Eight.)

Instruments from many cultures incorporate the 5-note pentatonic scale. With its name derived from the Greek *pente*, meaning five, and *tonic*, meaning tone, the pentatonic scale consists of five notes within an octave and is sometimes referred to as a 5-note scale. The sixth note played on the 5-hole Native American flute is the same as the fundamental note, but an octave higher. Pentatonic scales are common in modern folk music, music from Asian countries, and ancient European music.

While many early two-chamber native flutes were crafted with only five finger holes, a tradition continued by some crafters today, most modern Native American flutes feature six finger holes, with a hole in the blank space between a 5-hole flute's third and fourth holes. Players of the 6-hole flute generally keep the fourth finger hole closed, rendering the same primary scale as the 5-hole flutes. The 6-hole flute, however, offers broader playability by providing more achievable notes. A common problem with many 6-hole flutes, however, is that the octave-higher fundamental note plays sharp when the fourth finger hole remains closed while all others are open. If this occurs, open the fourth hole and close the fifth hole instead. In many cases, the flute will play the octave note correctly.

Scales

The following tables show finger positions for the pentatonic scale in clear columns and extended scale notes in shaded columns. Some notes can be achieved with alternate finger positions. Experiment and explore a particular flute's possibilities and limitations. To read the tables properly, the following guidelines apply:

- ➤ "X" represents a closed hole.
- ➤ "O" represents an open hole.
- ➤ "/" represents a hole that is half-closed/half-open.
- ➤ Hole 1 is the finger hole nearest to the flute's foot.
- ➤ Hole 6 is the finger hole nearest to the mouthpiece.
- ➤ Holes 1, 2, and 3 are covered with the right hand (unless left is preferred), using the third finger for hole 1, second finger for hole 2, first finger for hole 3.
- ➤ Holes 4, 5, and 6 are covered with the left hand's third, second, and first fingers respectively, unless you prefer to reverse hand position.

6-hole Chromatic Scale

Head

6	X	X	X	X	X	X	X	X	X	X	X	O	O	O
5	X	X	X	X	X	X	X	X	X	O	O	O	O	O
4	X	X	X	X	X	X	X	O	O	X	O	X	O	X
3	X	X	X	X	X	O	O	X	O	O	O	O	O	X
2	X	X	X	O	O	X	O	O	O	O	O	O	O	X
1	X	/	O	X	O	O	O	O	O	O	O	O	O	O

Foot   *   **   **

F#	G#	A	Bb	B	C	C#	D	Eb	E	F	F#	G	G#
G	A	Bb	B	C	C#	D	Eb	E	F	F#	G	G#	A
G#	Bb	B	C	C#	D	Eb	E	F	F#	G	G#	A	A#
A	B	C	C#	D	Eb	E	F	F#	G	G#	A	A#	B
Bb	C	C#	D	Eb	E	F	F#	G	G#	A	Bb	B	C
B	C#	D	Eb	E	F	F#	G	G#	A	Bb	B	C	C#
C	D	Eb	E	F	F#	G	G#	A	Bb	B	C	C#	D
C#	Eb	E	F	F#	G	G#	A	Bb	B	C	C#	D	Eb
D	E	F	F#	G	G#	A	Bb	B	C	C#	D	Eb	F
Eb	F	F#	G	G#	A	Bb	B	C	C#	D	Eb	F	F#
E	F#	G	G#	A	Bb	B	C	C#	D	Eb	F	F#	G
F	G	G#	A	Bb	B	C	C#	D	Eb	F	F#	G	G#

* Depending on the flute, this note may play sharp. If that happens, open hole 4 and cover hole 5 instead.

** These are easily achieved notes beyond the basic chromatic scale.

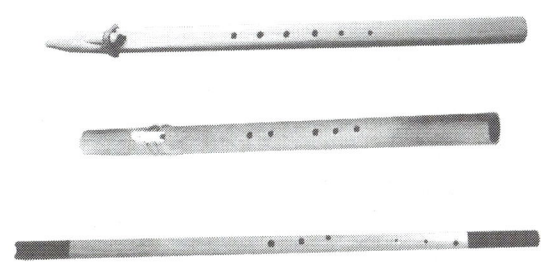

5-hole Chromatic Scale

The internet provides access to numerous fingering charts for 5- and 6-hole flutes. With some charts, however, extended scale notes can prove difficult or downright impossible. In some cases, extended scale finger positions render notes sharp or flat. If you encounter this problem, experiment by trying alternate fingerings, by varying coverage of a particular finger hole, or by varying the strength at which you blow. In the chart below, fingerings for the basic pentatonic scale appear in the clear columns and for extended scale notes in the shaded columns. Some of the extended notes are achieved by covering finger holes only halfway.

Head

5	X	X	X	X	X	X	X	X	X	X	/	O	O	O
4	X	X	X	X	X	X	X	/	O	O	O	O	O	O
3	X	X	X	X	X	/	O	O	X	O	O	O	X	X
2	X	X	X	/	O	O	O	O	O	O	O	O	X	X
1	X	/	O	O	O	O	O	O	O	O	O	O	X	O
Foot													**	**

F#	G#	A	Bb	B	C	C#	D	Eb	E	F	F#	G	G#
G	A	Bb	B	C	C#	D	Eb	E	F	F#	G	G#	A
G#	Bb	B	C	C#	D	Eb	E	F	F#	G	G#	A	A#
A	B	C	C#	D	Eb	E	F	F#	G	G#	A	A#	B
Bb	C	C#	D	Eb	E	F	F#	G	G#	A	Bb	B	C
B	C#	D	Eb	E	F	F#	G	G#	A	Bb	B	C	C#
C	D	Eb	E	F	F#	G	G#	A	Bb	B	C	C#	D
C#	Eb	E	F	F#	G	G#	A	Bb	B	C	C#	D	Eb
D	E	F	F#	G	G#	A	Bb	B	C	C#	D	Eb	F
Eb	F	F#	G	G#	A	Bb	B	C	C#	D	Eb	F	F#
E	F#	G	G#	A	Bb	B	C	C#	D	Eb	F	F#	G
F	G	G#	A	Bb	B	C	C#	D	Eb	F	F#	G	G#

** Easily achieved notes beyond the basic chromatic scale.

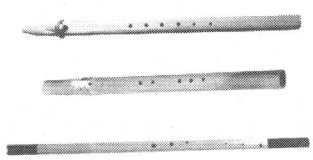

Anasazi Flute Scale

Clear columns in the following chart represent the primary scale for the Anasazi flute. Shaded columns represent extended scale notes. Some notes in the chart can be achieved by using alternate fingerings. Experiment to determine the limitations and potential of each flute. Hole 6 is the finger hole nearest to the blowing end. Hole 1 is the finger hole nearest to the foot.

Please note that the G# row represents the scale of the artifact flutes from Broken Flute Cave in Arizona. At a length of about 30 inches, finger hole spacing is uncomfortable for most play-ers and impossible for many others. However, by utilizing the size and percentage instructions in the Anasazi crafting section in Chapter Six, shorter flutes in higher keys can be crafted while remaining true to the ancient scale.

Unlike the modern two-chamber Native American flute, the Anasazi end-blown flute has the capability of two-plus octaves, similar to end- and side-blown flutes from other cultures. Playing higher octave notes can be achieved by narrowing lips to concentrate increased airflow across the blowing edge, utilizing the same fingerings of the lower octave.

Head

6	X	X	X	X	X	X	X	X	O
5	X	X	X	X	X	X	O	O	O
4	X	X	X	X	O	O	X	O	O
3	X	X	X	O	X	O	O	O	O
2	X	X	O	O	X	O	O	O	O
1	X	O	O	O	X	O	O	O	O

Foot

G#	Bb	B	C	D	Eb	E	F	G
A	B	C	C#	Eb	E	F	F#	G#
Bb	C	C#	D	E	F	F#	G	A
B	C#	D	Eb	F	F#	G	G#	Bb
C	D	Eb	E	F#	G	G#	A	B
C#	Eb	E	F	G	G#	A	Bb	C
D	E	F	F#	G#	A	Bb	B	C#
Eb	F	F#	G	A	Bb	B	C	D
E	F#	G	G#	Bb	B	C	C#	Eb
F	G	G#	A	B	C	C#	D	E
F#	G#	A	Bb	C	C#	D	Eb	F
G	A	Bb	B	C#	D	Eb	E	F#

Chapter Six

Crafting the Anasazi Flute

The ancient version of the Native American flute, more popularly known as the Anasazi flute, is arguably the easiest native flute to craft. Playing it, however, can prove quite difficult. Creating sound by directing air with your lips across a sharpened edge is far more challenging than playing an instrument that channels air across the labium for you. If you've never played an end-blown or traditional transverse flute, you'll need to either develop the ability before crafting or work with a flautist who can assist you throughout the crafting process.

Flute crafters and players alike have posted numerous instructional videos on their websites and on Youtube, which can be found easily through various search engines such as Google, with the search words "how to play the Anasazi flute." These videos offer a good alternative for instruction to persons who don't have access to experienced players. Although playing an

end-blown (edge-blown, rim-blown) flute is challenging, it is similar to coaxing a note from a bottle by blowing across the open end.

After crafting the blowing edge as described later in this chapter's crafting section, place the bottom part of the blowing end against the space between the lower lip and chin so it rests approximately at the bottom of the lower teeth. With pursed lips, direct air over the blowing edge at the top. Try tightening and loosening your lips and varying the airstream's force to produce a note. Vary the flute's tilt up and down to achieve the proper blowing angle.

Creating sound is dependent upon breath control, so don't be surprised or discouraged if you cannot create a note after a few minutes, hours, or even days. Try not to become frustrated. It can take a while. For lower notes, especially the fundamental note, blow more softly with lips slightly relaxed. To produce notes effectively, you'll need to experi-

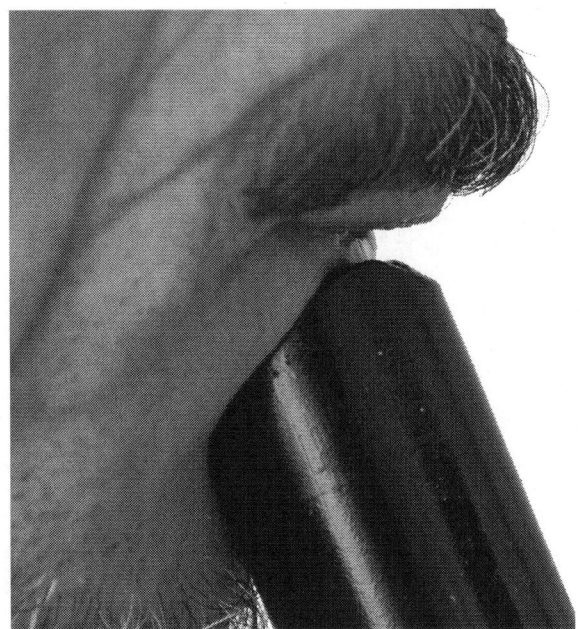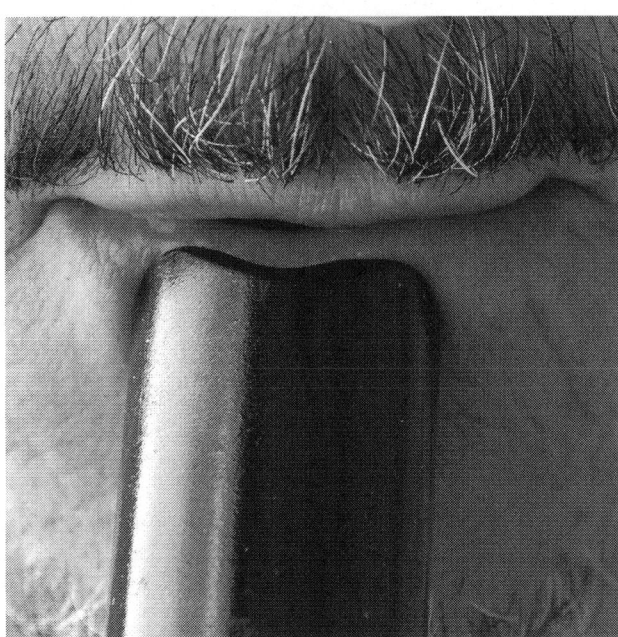

The space between the bottom lip and chin covers most of the flute's opening as the lips channel air across the sharpened blowing edge to create sound.

ment and practice. At some point, you'll create a sound. Remember how you did it and vary lip tightness, breath, angle, and pressure until you find the *sweet spot*. Once you've developed the skill to create a strong, steady note, proceed to the next step in crafting.

Materials

In general, crafters of the Anasazi flute choose wood for perceived sound quality and historical authenticity. Bamboo, however, makes a great and less labor intensive alternative. If you're new to crafting the ancient version, PVC provides an inexpensive and versatile choice for learning the basics before investing the time and energy required to craft a wooden or bamboo version. Be-

sides affordability, PVC is a superb medium for learning the craft and can result in a surprisingly good sounding instrument. Remember, though, always wear a high-quality dust mask or respirator when working with PVC.

If you've never crafted a flute before, you can develop and perfect technique with PVC, easily correcting mistakes that would ruin a more costly wood or bamboo attempt. For example, incorrect placement of finger holes is a common mistake for novice and experienced flute makers alike. (Some mistakes, such as incorrect finger hole placement, can be corrected with wood and bamboo as well. Such corrections are covered in Chapter Thirteen.) Correcting a misplaced hole on a PVC flute can be accomplished by covering it with tape, calculating correct placement, and drilling a new hole, resulting in a finished prototype. Note the finished prototype's measurements (length, hole placement, etc.) for use as a guide in crafting subsequent flutes, eliminating the need to calculate placement each time you craft a flute in that particular key and pipe size.

The biggest cost factor in crafting a wooden flute is the purchase or rental of required tools. To make the flute barrel, either a router or a wood lathe is required, the latter considerably more expensive but also more versatile, enabling crafters to drill the flute chamber and shape the barrel perfectly from a single piece of wood, creating a flute more uniform in appearance than those of the two-half router method. I don't own a lathe, nor do I have much experience in lathe use. I utilize the two-half method, routing each half carefully to form a specific diameter barrel when the two halves are glued together. If you work with a lathe, you most likely possess the knowledge and experience to create barrels in various diameters. Therefore, the following instructions for crafting with wood detail the two-half, routing method.

Craft the Anasazi Flute

Most Native American flutes—ancient, modern, traditional—are crafted from wood. Most crafters today make both the modern and ancient versions by utilizing the two-half method, routing channels in two pieces of wood.

The pieces are glued together to form the bore and flute body. Routing the two halves can be done either with chisels or an electric router-and-router-table setup, the method I prefer.

The Anasazi flute tuning scale, based on the scale of the artifact flutes, differs somewhat from the scale of the modern, two-chamber native flute. (See Chapter Five for more information on ancient and modern flute scales.) Based on the artifact flutes, starting with all finger holes closed and progressing toward the head from the finger hole closest to the foot, the tuning scale is G#, Bb, B, C, Eb, F, and G. Unlike the modern native flute's limited octave range, the Anasazi flute can achieve a full second octave when the player varies air flow and lip position and utilizes alternate finger positions.

The Anasazi flute employs the same tuning scale as the Andean *quena*. Unlike the *quena*, however, the Anasazi flute does not have a thumb hole on the bottom of the flute barrel. The Anasazi flute also is much longer than the *quena*, resulting in extreme gaps between finger holes, making the instrument especially challenging to play. With the instructions that follow, smaller versions of the flute can be crafted to provide players with smaller hands or restricted reach a playable instrument. Although in higher keys, the smaller flutes remain true to the original design and ancient scale.

Illustrations of the crafting process follow the directions.

Anasazi Tuning Scale

Key	Hole 1	Hole 2	Hole 3	Hole 4	Hole 5	Hole 6
G#	Bb	B	C	Eb	F	G
A	B	C	C#	E	F#	G#
Bb	C	C#	D	F	G	A
B	C#	D	Eb	F#	G#	Bb
C	D	Eb	E	G	A	B
C#	Eb	E	F	G#	Bb	C
D	E	F	F#	A	B	C#
Eb	F	F#	G	Bb	C	D
E	F#	G	G#	B	C#	Eb
F	G	G#	A	C	D	E
F#	G#	A	Bb	C#	Eb	F
G	A	Bb	B	D	E	F#

Anasazi Wooden Flute

Materials

- 1/2 x 4 x 36-inch hobby board (available in pine, poplar, oak, and other woods, depending on store stock) or 1/2 x 4 x 36-inch aromatic cedar plank, usually a mail-order item
- carpenter's glue
- fine, medium, coarse sandpaper
- finishing oil (Danish, teak, linseed, tung oil, etc.)
- spray lacquer or paint (optional)

Tools

- electronic chromatic tuner (tuning applications for computers and smartphones provide an excellent alternative to a stand-alone tuner)
- electric sander (optional)
- tape measure
- small handsaw or hacksaw
- electric table saw (optional)
- straightedge at least 36 inches long
- 4 to 8 wood clamps such as C-clamps or bar clamps
- 3-inch trimming hand plane
- electric router
- router table
- 3/4-inch core box router bit
- rotary tool (high-speed drill

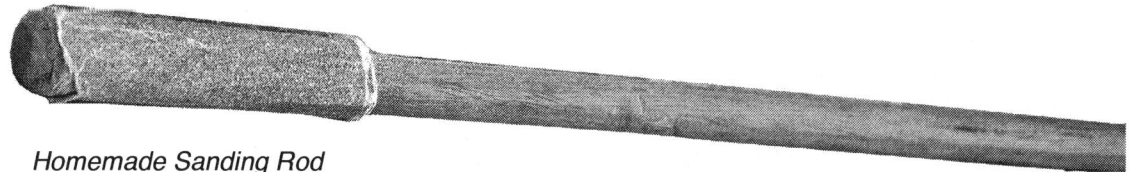

Homemade Sanding Rod

1. *Slit one end of the dowel the width of the sanding paper.*
2. *Insert one end of the sandpaper.*
3. *Wrap the sheet of sandpaper around the dowel, rough side out.*
4. *To better secure the paper, apply glue to the underside of the final layer.*
5. *Secure by wrapping with a rubber band to ensure the exterior layer's underside maintains contact with the interior layer.*
6. *Allow to dry before use.*

can suffice with wood)
- 1/8-inch drill bit
- 1/4-inch flat and rounded needle files
- flat fine-tooth wood file
- homemade sanding rod: 1/2-inch to 5/8-inch dowel, ends wrapped with sandpaper (see above)

Router Setup

1. Attach the router to the router table according to manufacturer instructions.

2. Mark the wood to be routed for a bit height of 3/8-inch.

3. Place the wood on the router table against the router bit.

4. Adjust the router bit up or down so the router tip rests at the mark on the wood.

5. Set the router cutting guide to ensure at least 1/4-inch between the guide and channel wall.

Craft the Wood Flute

1. Rout the wood from end to end. Flip the wood around or over to rout the second channel.

2. With a table saw or handsaw, split the wood between the two channels, making sure that at least 1/4-inch of wood remains between the cut and channel walls.

3. Sand the interior channel halves to ensure a smooth sur-

face. Wrap fine-grade sand-paper around a dowel for uniformity. Sand *only* the channel interior and not the top of the channels where the two halves will be joined.

4. Apply a thin layer of glue to the points where the two halves will contact to achieve good adhesion and prevent air leaks when dry.

5. Match the halves together to form a 3/4-inch diameter barrel.

6. Clamp the flute and allow at least 24 hours to dry.

7. With the small hand plane, rough-shape the wood into a conventional flute barrel. Around the bore on each end, draw a circle for the desired thickness (1/8-inch to 1/4-inch). With the hand plane, plane to the desired thickness a length of about two inches from each end. Then shape the middle section to the thickness of the ends.

8. By hand, sheet sander, rotary sander (such as a drill with sanding attachment), or bench sander, fine shape the barrel, rounding it as best as possible, beginning with coarse paper, followed by medium and fine grade paper.

9. Shape the blowing edge. (Some crafters prefer to shape one side of the barrel into a blowing edge without any other alteration to the mouthpiece end. I prefer the blowing end to be cut at a 25-degree angle for comfort and better air control.) With a fine-tooth flat wood file, shape the blowing edge roughly to a 45-degree angle. As the edge sharpens, a "C" shape will appear and deepen. Keep the indentation to a depth of no more than 1/4-inch. The blowing edge should be sharp. To get it as sharp as possible, use fine-grade sandpaper.

10. Clean away dust and fragments from the flute and blowing edge. Test the flute by producing a note. Practice until you can sustain the flute's fundamental note. Then proceed to the next step.

11. Decide whether you'll craft the standard length Anasazi, which will be around 30 inches, or a shorter version. With the tuner, determine the initial fundamental note. At 36 inches, the pipe's pitch should be lower than G#. Shorten the barrel in small increments to raise the fundamental to the desired pitch, cutting off no more than 1/4-inch to 1/2-inch each time, testing after each cut.

12. With a straightedge, draw a line from the middle of the blowing edge to the flute's foot to act as a guide in placing finger holes.

13. Determine finger hole placement.

Flute Length x Percentage = Hole Position

With hole 1 the closest to the flute's foot and farthest from the labium, use the above formula and the following percentages to calculate placement of each hole by measuring from the labium:

- hole 1 at 84 percent from labium
- hole 2 at 78 percent
- hole 3 at 72 percent
- hole 4 at 60 percent
- hole 5 at 55 percent
- hole 6 at 49 percent

14. According to calculations, mark the barrel for finger holes. Long flutes can be played more easily if the finger holes are drilled off-center, with holes 1 and 2 to the right of center and holes 5 and 6 to the left of center.

15. Drill hole 1 no larger than 1/8-inch. Determine hole pitch. It should be lower than desired. With a half-round or round needle file, raise the pitch by enlarging the hole very slightly, primarily toward the sides and blowing edge, testing frequently until the desired pitch has been attained. Proceed to the remaining holes, bringing each to the desired pitch before proceeding to the next.

16. Remove any hole fragments with fine sandpaper. Do not enlarge holes any further after attaining correct pitch.

17. Fine-sand the flute's interior and exterior. Use the homemade sanding rod for the interior. Apply pre-finish if desired, including stain or oil such as tung or linseed. If applying oil or stain, allow 24 hours to dry before proceeding to the final step.

18. With a clean cloth, remove remaining dust from the flute's interior and exterior. Finish the flute as desired. I prefer spray lacquer, applying it first to the interior barrel. After drying (usually 45 minutes is sufficient), apply a light coat to the exterior. Do not over-spray, causing uneven distribution. Apply a second coat after the first has dried sufficiently. Allow the final application to dry for at least 24 hours.

Craft the Anasazi Wooden Flute Illustrated

Rout first channel, end to end.

Rout second channel.

Rip plank to separate channels.

Fine-sand channel. Do not sand channel rim.

With oil-damp cloth, clean channels.

Apply glue to contact points of both channels.

Assemble channels to form bore.

Clamp and allow 24 hours to dry.

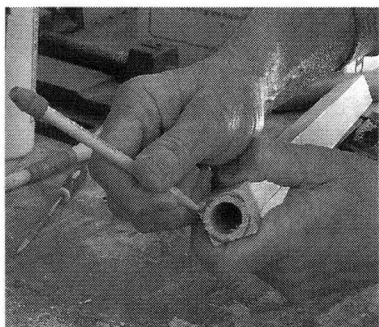

After drying, mark plane guideline around bore on each end.

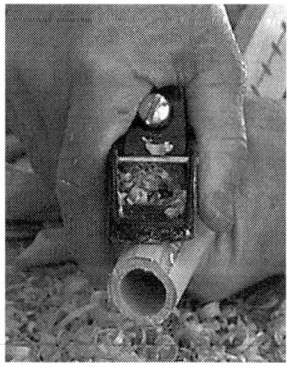

Plane each end to guide marks.

Rough plane the rest of the flute to match planed ends.

File mouthpiece end at 45-degree angle to create blowing edge.

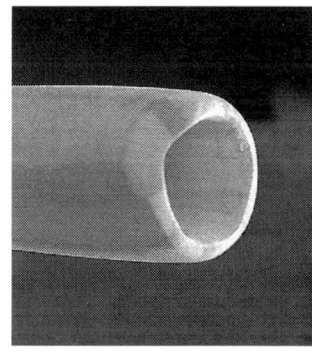

The rough-cut blowing edge.

After establishing the fundamental, measure and mark for finger holes. Mark holes 1, 2, 5, and 6 off-center for better reach.

Drill and shape holes one by one, tuning each to proper pitch before moving to the next.

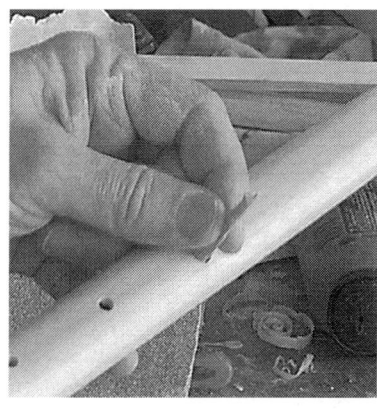

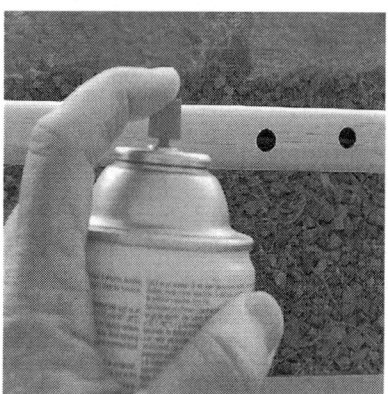

Fine-sand finger holes.

Fine-sand flute interior and exterior.

Finish with oil, lacquer, or paint as desired.

Anasazi Bamboo Flute

Materials

- ❧ 32-inch length of bamboo with an internal bore of approximately 3/4-inch
- ❧ fine, medium, coarse sandpaper
- ❧ finishing oil (Danish, linseed, tung oil, etc.)
- ❧ spray lacquer (optional)

Tools

- ❧ electronic chromatic tuner (tuning applications for computers and smartphones provide an excellent alternative to a stand-alone tuner)
- ❧ electric sander (optional)
- ❧ tape measure
- ❧ straightedge at least three feet long
- ❧ small handsaw or hacksaw
- ❧ rotary tool (a standard power drill to make holes can easily split bamboo, rendering the selected piece useless)
- ❧ 1/8-inch drill bit for rotary tool
- ❧ electric drill
- ❧ 16-inch to 18-inch extra-long drill bit (slightly smaller diameter than bamboo bore)
- ❧ flat and rounded needle files, no wider than 1/4-inch
- ❧ flat fine-tooth wood file
- ❧ homemade sanding rod: 1/2-inch to 5/8-inch dowel, ends wrapped with sandpaper (refer to image and directions in Anasazi wooden flute section)

Craft the Flute

Crafting the Anasazi flute with bamboo includes two steps not required in crafting flutes from wood. Photos for the steps unique to bamboo are included here. Illustrations for general steps are included in the preceding wood flute section.

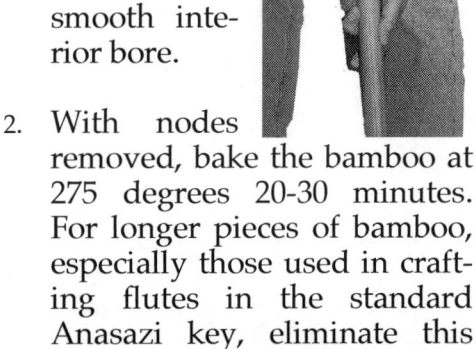

1. With the drill and the extra-long bit, carefully remove bamboo nodes to create a tube. Sand interior node areas with the homemade sanding rod to ensure a smooth interior bore.

2. With nodes removed, bake the bamboo at 275 degrees 20-30 minutes. For longer pieces of bamboo, especially those used in crafting flutes in the standard Anasazi key, eliminate this step since long pieces will not

fit into a conventional oven. Baking causes the bamboo's oils to create a natural gloss finish similar to lacquer. However, some of this finish will be sanded off during the drilling and finishing stages.

3. Using the same method described in the preceding wooden flute section, cut the blowing end with a fine-tooth handsaw at a 25-degree angle. Use a fine-tooth flat wood file to shape the blowing edge to a roughly 45-degree angle. As the edge sharpens, a "C" or oval shape will form. Try to keep the indentation to a depth of no more than 1/4-inch. The blowing edge should be sharp. Sharpen the edge with fine-grade sandpaper.

4. Clean the flute and blowing edge carefully of all dust. Practice blowing until you can produce a sustained low note on the flute.

5. Decide whether you'll craft the standard size Anasazi, about 30 inches in length, or a shorter version. With the tuner, determine the initial fundamental note. The pipe's pitch should be lower than G#. Shorten the barrel in small increments to the desired pitch, cutting off no more than 1/4-inch to 1/2-inch each time, testing after each cut.

6. With a straightedge, draw a line from middle of the blowing edge to the flute's foot to use as a guide in placing finger holes.

7. Bore diameter will vary between different pieces of bamboo. It's unlikely you'll find a bore that is exactly 3/4-inch diameter, but that's okay. The percentages to determine finger-hole placement work for bores of different diameters.

Flute Length x Percentage = Hole Position

With hole 1 the closest to the flute's foot and farthest from the labium, use the following percentages in the above formula to calculate and mark the placement for each hole by measuring from the labium:

- hole 1 at 84 percent from labium
- hole 2 at 78 percent
- hole 3 at 72 percent
- hole 4 at 60 percent
- hole 5 at 55 percent
- hole 6 at 49 percent

8. Along the guideline, mark where each finger hole should be placed as calculated. Place finger holes off-center for easier reach on longer flutes, with holes 1 and 2 to the right of center and holes 5 and 6 to the left of center.

9. Use a high-speed rotary tool to drill holes. A conventional

drill can easily split the bamboo. Drill hole 1 no larger than 1/8-inch. Do not proceed to the next hole. Determine hole 1's pitch, which should be lower than desired. With a half-round or round needle file, raise the pitch by enlarging the hole incrementally, primarily toward the sides and blowing edge, testing frequently until the desired pitch has been attained. Proceed to the remaining holes, bringing each to desired pitch before going to the next.

10. Remove fragments from finger holes with fine sandpaper. Do not enlarge a hole any further after tuning it to correct pitch.

11. Fine-sand both the interior and exterior of the flute. Use the homemade sanding rod for the interior. If desired, apply an oil finish, such as tung or linseed. Allow to dry for 24 hours before proceeding to the final step.

12. With a clean cloth, remove dust from the interior and exterior. Finish the flute with paint or lacquer if desired. I prefer spray lacquer, available in assorted colors, including clear and black, applying it first to the interior barrel. After sufficient drying (usually 45 minutes), apply a thin coat to the exterior. Take care not to over-spray, especially the blowing end. Over-spraying can cause runs or a "lumpy" finish which, if on the blowing edge, can hamper sound production. Apply a second coat after the first has dried. Allow the final coat to dry for at least 24 hours.

Anasazi PVC Flute

Materials

- 3/4-inch diameter PVC pipe, 32 inches long
- fine sandpaper
- fine steel wool
- spray lacquer or paint (optional)

Tools

- electronic chromatic tuner (with available apps, a computer or smartphone can be an excellent alternative to a stand-alone tuner)
- tape measure
- straightedge at least 36 inches long
- small handsaw or hacksaw
- rotary tool
- 1/8-inch drill bit
- flat and rounded needle files, no wider than 1/4-inch
- flat fine-tooth wood file

Craft the Flute

1. Cut the blowing end with a fine-tooth handsaw at a 25-degree angle. Use a fine-tooth flat wood file to shape the blowing edge to a roughly 45-

degree angle. As the edge sharpens, a "C" or oval shape will form. Try to keep the indentation to a depth of no more than 1/4-inch. Finish the edge with fine-grade sandpaper.

2. Clean dust and remnants carefully from the blowing edge. Practice until you produce a sustained low note on the flute.

3. With the tuner, determine the initial fundamental note. The pipe's pitch should be lower than G#. Decide whether you'll craft the standard size Anasazi, which will be around 30 inches in length, or a shorter version. Shorten the barrel in small increments to the desired pitch, cutting off no more than 1/4-inch each time, testing after each cut.

4. With a straightedge, draw a line from the middle of the blowing edge to the flute's foot to act as a guide in placing finger holes.

5. Use the following formula and percentages to determine placement:

Flute Length x Percentage = Hole Position

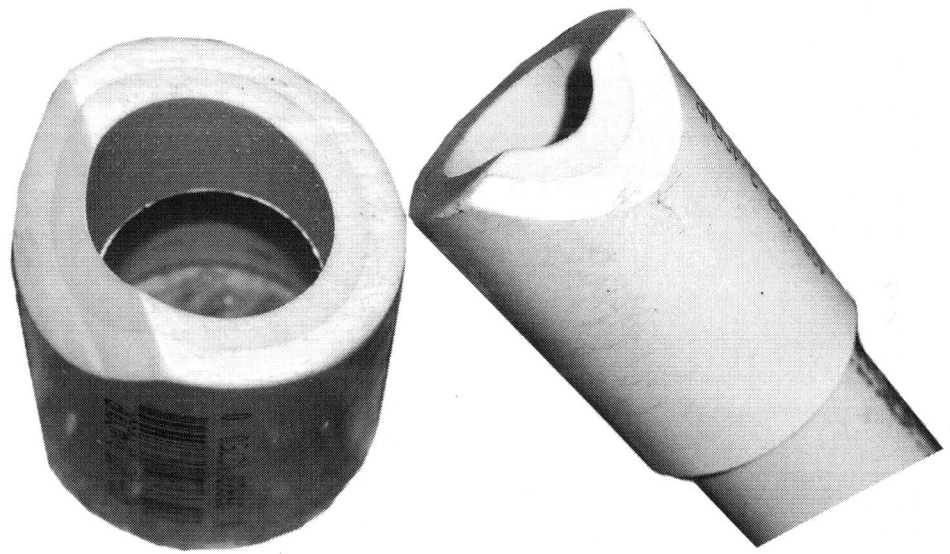

Alternative blowing edge: *A PVC blowing edge can be crafted and used on multiple barrels.*

1. *With a 3/4-inch pipe connector, insert a PVC pipe into one end until it fits snugly against the connector's midpoint lip.*
2. *Cut the barrel flush with the connector.*
3. *Shape the blowing edge as described in the Anasazi wooden flute crafting section.*

This blowing edge can be slipped onto PVC barrels to craft and play multiple flutes, including Anasazi and others such as shakuhachi.

With hole 1 the closest to the flute's foot, mark the placement for each finger hole by measuring from the labium:

- hole 1 at 84 percent from labium
- hole 2 at 78 percent
- hole 3 at 72 percent
- hole 4 at 60 percent
- hole 5 at 55 percent
- hole 6 at 49 percent

6. Mark hole placement along the guideline as calculated. Place finger holes off-center for easier reach on longer flutes, with holes 1 and 2 to the right of center and holes 5 and 6 to the left of center.

7. Use a high-speed rotary tool to drill holes. Drill hole 1 no larger than 1/8-inch. Do not proceed to the next hole. Determine hole 1's pitch, which should be lower than desired.

With a half-round or round needle file, raise the pitch by enlarging the hole incrementally, primarily toward the sides and labium, testing frequently until the desired pitch has been attained. Proceed to the remaining holes one by one, bringing each to the desired pitch before proceeding to the next.

8. Fine-sand each hole to remove fragments. Do not enlarge holes further.

9. Scrub the PVC with fine grade steel wool and a gentle cleansing product to remove factory markings. Rinse. Dry the interior and exterior.

10. Finish the flute with spray lacquer or spray paint if desired.

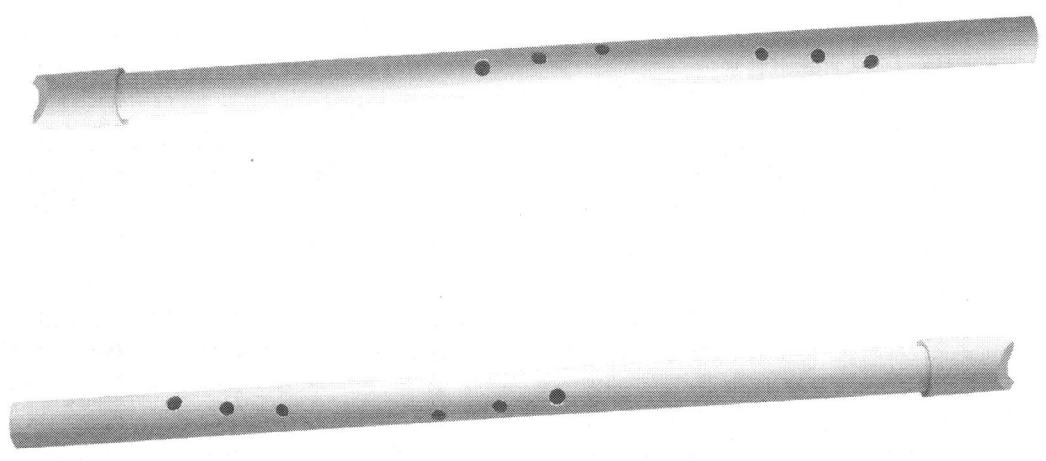

Chapter Seven

The Fetish (Bird)

As mentioned in Chapter One, the Native American *flute* is technically a whistle with two separate chambers. A channel directs air flow from the air chamber hole to the sound hole where it's split by the labium to create sound. The channel can be carved into the flute body or the underside of the fetish (also known as the block, totem, or bird) that sits atop the flute, or created by a spacer of wood, metal, or plastic between the fetish and flute body.

Some historians and flute aficionados believe early flautists directed air flow from the air hole to sound hole with a finger instead of a bird. If that's the case, it's unlikely the flute body had more than four finger holes since one hand would be occupied with guiding air.

Most artifact flutes in private and museum collections employ some kind of air block, from early flutes that utilize a strap of leather wrapped around the flute body to 19th century and later flutes that employ wooden blocks, commonly thin and of no particular design. From the late 1800s to present, the bird has evolved as a work of art that runs the gamut of primitive designs to intricately detailed, museum quality carvings. Nevertheless, no matter the artistic design or shape, the bird is designed to do one job specifically—guide air from the slow air chamber to the labium to create sound.

As the bird took on more ornate, artistic design, especially during the mid- to late-1900s, the term *fetish* became the more commonly used due to the increasing popularity of carving the air block in the image of animals, many used as traditional fetishes in Native American cultures, especially the Zuni. A traditional fetish is considered a magical charm or talisman possessed with special powers. In native cultures, fetishes usually take the form of an animal

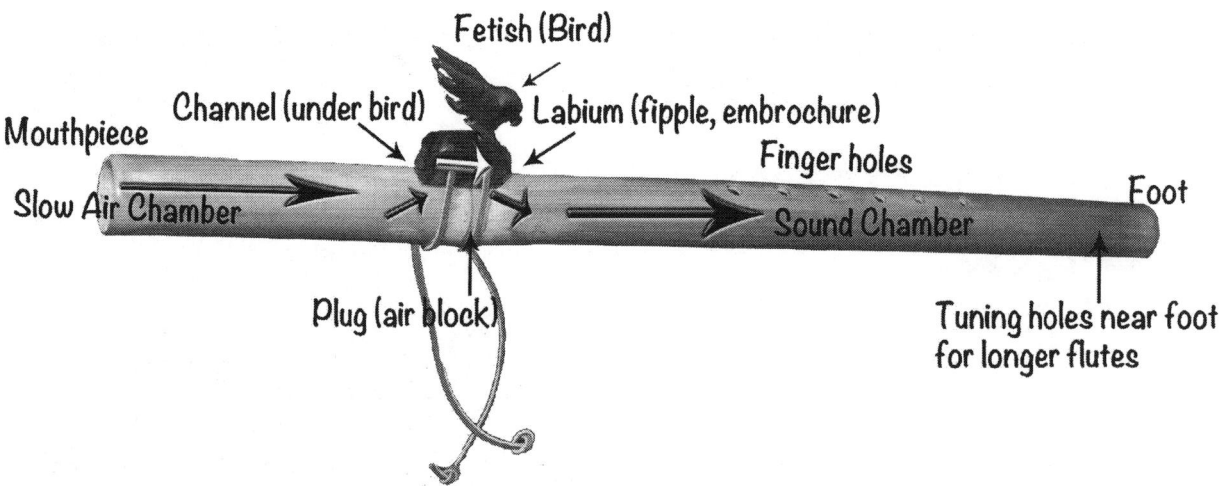

Fetish (Bird)

Channel (under bird)   Labium (fipple, embrochure)

Mouthpiece   Finger holes

Slow Air Chamber   Sound Chamber   Foot

Plug (air block)

Tuning holes near foot
for longer flutes

or specific god and are believed to enhance the abilities or good fortune of a person or family. The majority of carved birds on today's Native American flutes are not fetishes in the literal sense, only artistically carved figures. An *authentic* fetish must be blessed by a priest or shaman. With proper blessing, all birds can become true fetishes.

Flute makers craft fetishes—carving in the traditional hand-tool method or with the use of modern tools—from a variety of materials, including clay, wood, and various stones such as turquoise. The most common material is wood, a medium that is both easy to work with and durable. Some crafters make fetishes from two or three pieces of material, with the lower section incorporating the channel and serving as the base for the carved animal figure, whether wooden or stone. Although most native flute fetishes are a flute's primary decoration, some crafters are such adept carvers that the flute itself becomes an elaborate extension of the small fetish it supports.

In many native cultures, animals are believed to be spirit guides who appear in dreams or during vision quests. They professedly accompany people through-

out life, providing guidance and protection. The majority of animals depicted as fetishes are those that prey on others, traditionally admired for their skills to survive and conquer. Some of the most popular include the bear, wolf, and eagle. For use as flute birds, however, the range of images is limited only by player desire and crafter ability. Many players choose animals special to them, from cats to dolphins, from hummingbirds to dragonflies. No matter the animal and depending on the native culture, the carved image usually carries a special meaning or interpretation. In the Zuni culture, for example, a bear is considered introspective and strong, while a buffalo represents endurance and emotional courage. A butterfly represents transformation, while the snake represents death and rebirth. The primary purpose of any fetish, whether on a flute or as a stand-alone work of art, is to counter the problems in life, whether they're physical or mental.

The earliest fetishes were not crafted by hand, but formed naturally in stone and selected because they resembled certain animals. While most native cultures, especially those in the southwest, utilized fetishes in various aspects of

Above, a pre-1900 whistle from the Blackfoot tribe. Photo courtesy of the Dayton C. Miller Flute Collection, Library of Congress, Music Division. Below, a pre-1900 Plains Indians flute, utilizing a metal spacer for channeling air. Photo courtesy of The Brooklyn Museum.

daily life, the Zuni nation is the culture best known for its use and production of fetishes. Historically, fetishes were coveted objects for their believed powers to bring better luck in hunting, medicine, fertility, and planting, employed in an endless assortment of personal uses including protection.

Since animals, objects, and nature are believed to have a type of *spirit power* that can either help or hinder humans, native people believed that carved fetishes harnessed and possessed the same spiritual force as the animals they represented, that those forces could be used to the advantage of those who owned the specific fetishes. Owners would often equip a fetish with a representative bundle of coral or turquoise or an arrowhead tied to its side or back as an offering for future blessings or in thanks of favors or blessings already received. Some carvings incorporate turquoise or coral inlay from the mouth to the center of the body, usually as an arrow, representing the *heart line*, the breath and life force. The creation and sale of fetishes

today has become a major economical endeavor for some native cultures, especially the Zuni.

While traditional fetishes were restricted to animal images, today's native flute birds depict almost anything. The offering of many crafters is broad with very little off-limits. If tradition is the goal, however, the following animals are those most commonly represented by traditional fetishes.

- **Badger**: The badger represents assertiveness and persistence. While believed to have some healing powers, the badger imbues the ability to focus on accomplishing a specific goal or purpose.
- **Bat**: Due to its ability to fly, the bat represents the ability to create and influence dreams. It offers new perspectives, represented by sleeping upside down in caves. Flying into and out of caves represents a shamanic journey into death and initiation. The bat's sonar suggests the talent to see and hear hidden messages

from the Great Spirit, messages invisible to those with normal sight and hearing.

Bear: The bear provides a variety of blessings, including strength and enhanced abilities in parenting, hunting, healing, and protection. Hibernation denotes inner knowledge and exploration. The bear has proved one of the most popular fetishes in all generations.

Beaver: The beaver represents a cooperative attitude, coupled with purpose and drive. Due to its mating and family habits, the beaver symbolizes devotion to family and home.

Bison: The buffalo, most important to Plains Indians, is a spiritual entity connected to the traditional smoking of the pipe. Due in part to its massive size, it's associated with abundance, consistency, blessings, prosperity, strength, and gratitude. A white bison is particularly revered in native mythology, promising future prosperity.

Bobcat: Bobcats are known for independence and an ability to penetrate and transcend boundaries. Rarely spotted due to their nocturnal nature, bobcats, unlike many other felines, will pursue their prey into bodies of water.

Butterfly: The butterfly, developing from egg to caterpillar to butterfly, represents transformation and the importance of each stage of development. The butterfly inhabits the air realm, symbolic of the mind and its ability to transcend the physical world with thought.

Coyote: The coyote is considered a trickster by many native cultures. It represents the unpredictable nature of life paired with the ability to contend with and profit from the unex-

pected by focusing on the moment rather than the past or future.

Deer: The deer symbolizes great sensitivity and gentleness, superior agility, and an extraordinary ability to survive lopsided odds.

Dragonfly: The dragonfly is considered a spiritual messenger who carries prayers into the spirit world. It's designated as a water sign because it lays its eggs in water. The dragonfly is an agile creature, able to move quickly in any direction. Referred to as the Pueblo Cross, its iridescent or varied colored wings imply that human perception of reality is an illusion.

Eagle: The eagle's keen sight over great distances represents extraordinary vision in common existence, an ability to comprehend the complete picture in a given situation. The eagle also signifies life as a physical and spiritual journey.

Elk: The elk is known for its stamina and ability to outlast its prey. Considered by many native cultures as a warrior, the elk possesses great stamina, power, and sense of brotherhood and sisterhood.

Fox: The fox is a clever entity who easily conceals itself in its surroundings to avoid danger. Its ability to outwit predators and blend with its surroundings underscores a perceived connection to the supernatural and an ability to shape-shift. A fox fetish bestows self-restraint, discretion, and adaptability to anything good for the self or clan.

Frog: A sign of water, the frog epitomizes life, cleansing, and emotional and physical healing.

Hawk: The hawk belongs more to the physical world than the eagle, bearing messages between people and animals rather than messages to the spirit world. It stands for vigilance and constant awareness of surroundings.

- **Horse**: Providing people fast transportation and the ability to move heavy loads, the horse represents power, mobility, and freedom. The horse enjoys a special connection with humans that does not exist with any other animal.
- **Hummingbird**: The hummingbird is fast and colorful, able to migrate vast distances while surviving on sweet nectar. The hummingbird symbolizes an open and caring heart and the ready ability to experience love and joy.
- **Kolowisi**: The Zuni Pueblo culture's Kolowisi is a mythical water serpent, usually feathered or horned. Unlike the evil serpent in the Christian Garden of Eden, the Kolowisi is a hero who saved the Zuni from the great flood by delivering food and other items needed to sustain life and flourish after flood waters receded. Kolowisi is the guardian of water sources and is said to live in the Rio Grande and in underground streams of the southwest.
- **Lizard**: The lizard, with its ability to lose and regrow its tail, symbolizes the ability to survive. Its habit of sunbathing while remaining extremely alert exemplifies the ability to focus on dreams and visions while remaining connected to reality.
- **Mole**: Considered a guardian of nature and earth, the mole embodies the trust of intuition and feelings rather than trusting only what the eye sees.
- **Mountain lion**: A great hunter and leader, the mountain lion possesses extraordinary ability in perceiving, understanding, and respecting its boundaries, setting good examples to others.
- **Mouse**: The mouse is inquisitive and energetic, with a keen ability to confront, understand, and address that which is immediately before it. The mouse quickly focuses on the specific details required to alleviate a problem.
- **Owl**: Considered wise in many cultures, the owl is both a physical and spiritual being with an inner source of understanding. It represents a clairvoyant ability to reveal deception in others.
- **Rabbit**: Small and seemingly defenseless, the rabbit is reflexively quick with keen senses for survival, readily acknowledging but refusing to allow its fears to paralyze it or dictate self-destructive behavior.
- **Raven**: Another trickster in many native mythologies, the raven is known for its ability to transform itself or its surroundings. It symbolizes an ability to change consciousness to discover and deal with fears that hinder progress, converting anger and fear into positive emotional power to attain success.
- **Snake**: Shedding its skin as it grows, the snake symbolizes the ability to discard the past, destructive behaviors, and false perceptions, transforming the negative into positive.
- **Spider**: With its ability to spin silk, the spider represents a connection between all things large and small, good and bad in the great web of existence.
- **Turkey**: Raised by Pueblo Indians, the turkey became a symbol of nature's gifts and resources. The turkey is a reminder to honor and nurture nature and to understand that giving

for the benefit of all increases personal fortune.

- **Turtle**: Like the turkey, the turtle is a reminder to respect the earth and nature. Carrying its home in the form of a shell, the turtle teaches *to go with the flow*, to use whatever life brings to one's advantage rather than fighting against it.
- **Wolf**: The wolf represents individuality and the importance of the clan. Its wisdom is defined by an ability to use new information to benefit both clan and self. Even so, the wolf never allows itself to be blinded by clan loyalty.

Some of the early birds I carved. In recent years, I've employed a simple image for birds, concentrating solely on sound quality rather than detailed carving.

Over the years, I've carved a variety of animals, including wolves, bears, dolphins, horses, hummingbirds, and more. I am not a native shaman, medicine man, or member of any Native American tribe, nor have I had these carvings blessed by native holy people to empower them as fetishes in the true sense of the word. Add to that, I am not a highly-skilled carver. Each carving involved much more time than making the actual flute. To compensate properly for time put into carving the bird and crafting the flute, the finished product would have to be quite expensive. Therefore, I've left custom carving behind to concentrate on crafting the best-sounding flutes I can make, equipping them with generic birds, usually rectangular with softened edges or in an ab-

stract "bird" shape, resulting in flutes that resemble those from the 1800s.

The instructions that follow detail crafting a bird for sound. The directions are the same whether you're crafting a nondescript bird or an ornate, intricate carving.

A word of caution: If you decide to carve the channel into the flute body, take great care. I've discarded numerous flutes due to crafting the channel improperly. It's much easier and less wasteful to discard a fetish that won't work than a flute that's been marred beyond repair.

Perhaps the easiest fetish to craft is a slide-on fetish for a PVC flute, crafted from a PVC pipe connector that's been split (see photo on next page). Take extra care in creating the nest on a PVC flute if you plan to use a slide-on fetish. (Directions follow in the crafting section.) After fashioning the slide-on fetish, flatten the nest area on the flute barrel in small increments, testing the sound frequently. Otherwise, the nest area may become too flat for the fetish to channel air properly, much the same way a channel in a fetish or on the barrel can be cut too deep to provide good sound. If the nest becomes too flat, the slide-on fetish will have to be discarded in favor of a conventional bird.

When fashioning conventional birds, some crafters prefer to cut the air

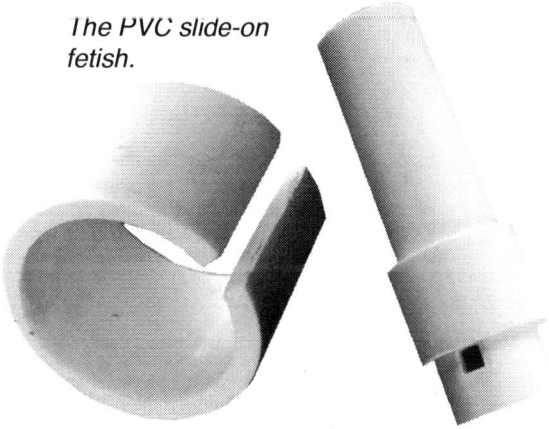

The PVC slide-on fetish.

channel into the body of the flute despite the potential hazard of ruining the instrument. I prefer to cut the channel into the bottom of the fetish because a channel in the fetish affords greater leeway for correcting mistakes in channel depth or form. When cutting the channel into the flute body, crafters sometimes taper both top and bottom of the sound hole's splitting edge (labium). With the channel in the bottom of the fetish, crafters need to taper only the bottom of the labium, again allowing for easier correction of mistakes. I've had only moderate success when carving the channel into the flute body. In some cases, I've had no choice but to discard flutes rendered unusable due to mistakes and attempted corrections. If you have considerable experience with power tools, especially routers in doing fine-detailed, shallow work, you may prefer to carve the channel into the barrel since it will allow use of a variety of birds—anything flat, wide, and long enough to cover the nest area from the air hole to the sound hole. If you don't have the expertise and access to precise woodworking tools, the following instructions detail how to craft a fetish that incorporates the channel.

Craft the Bird/Fetish

The bird is the smallest and one of the most crucial aspects of crafting a Native American flute. I usually craft the fetish after drilling and shaping the air and sound holes. For PVC, the following photos feature a slide-on fetish crafted for a large-bore flute.

The PVC Slide-on Bird

Materials & Tools

- PVC pipe connector for specific PVC flute size
- fine-tooth handsaw
- rounded and flat needle files for smaller diameters; rounded wood file for larger diameters
- fine grade sandpaper

Craft the Fetish

1. Determine whether to use the entire connector or to cut it for a shorter fit. Make certain it is long enough to cover from at least 1/4-inch behind the air hole (the mouthpiece side) to the back edge (mouthpiece side) of the sound hole.

2. Cut one side of the connector lengthwise. This will be the bottom.

3. With a needle file or wood file, remove the connector's interior divider lip to create a smooth interior bore.

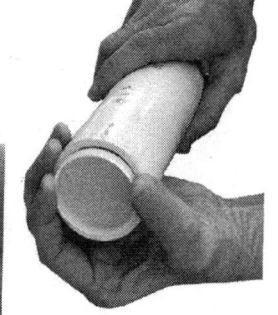

4. Smooth with fine-grade sand-paper.

The Wood Fetish

Materials

- ❧ wood (popular softwoods include pine and cedar; popular hardwoods include ebony and maple), at least 2 x 2 x 1-inch, long enough to cover the air chamber hole to the mouthpiece side of the sound hole and tall enough to accommodate any planned carved figure
- ❧ if preferred to carving the channel, 1/32-inch or 1/16-inch thick hobby board to act as spacer or to form channel on fetish bottom
- ❧ carpenter's glue
- ❧ fine and medium sandpaper
- ❧ finishing oil (linseed, tung oil, etc.)
- ❧ spray lacquer (optional)
- ❧ two 12-inch leather strings, twine, or other material for securing the fetish to the flute

Tools

- ❧ fine-tooth saw or coping saw
- ❧ X-ACTO™ knife (for use with hobby wood as spacer)
- ❧ 1/4-inch chisel for carving channel into fetish or flute barrel
- ❧ needle files

Craft the Wood Fetish

When carving an animal or other figure, save the carving step for last if the channel will be part of the bird design. A finished 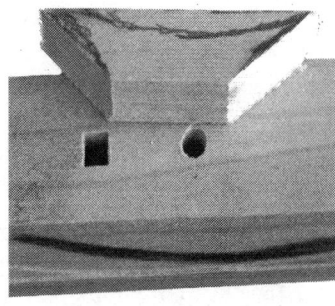 carving is more easily broken than a blank when chiseling the channel. If the channel is carved into the flute body or created by a stand-alone spacer, carving the fetish design can be first or last. In any case, make sure the base of the bird is appropriately sized for the flute to which it will be attached.

1. Optional: Notch one end of the bird approximately 1/4-inch wide and 1/4-inch deep to create a flue. In my experience, a flue can improve sound on some flutes while degrading sound on others.

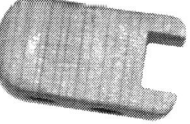

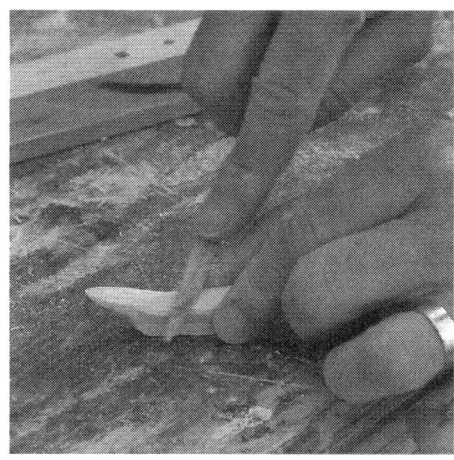

2. If you are not carving a custom fetish, rough-shape the bird and sand the bottom flat.

3. To cut the channel into the bird or flute body:

   a. When cutting the channel into the bird, mark its underside the length from the mouthpiece edge of the sound hole to 1/4-inch beyond the mouthpiece side of air hole. Draw guide marks for a 1/4-inch channel.

   b. When cutting the channel into the flute body, mark guides for a 1/4-inch wide channel from the sound hole to the air hole.

   c. Chisel a shallow channel no more than 1-16-inch in the bird or flute body.

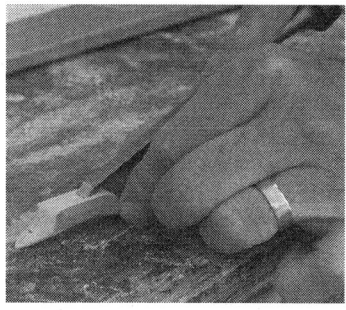

   d. Level and smooth the channel with a flat needle file and fine-grade sandpaper. Test for sound. Make adjustments as required. If the channel is in the flute body, do not make the initial channel deep. A channel chiseled too deep into the flute body can render the flute useless.

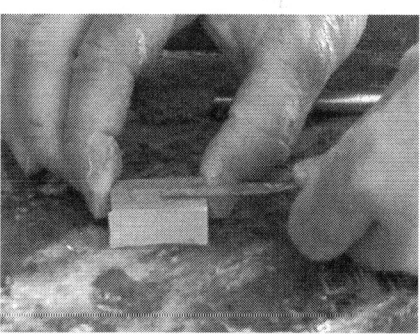

4. If you prefer to use a spacer attached to the bird's underside:

   a. Place the bird on the 1/32"-thick hobby board, and mark the wood.

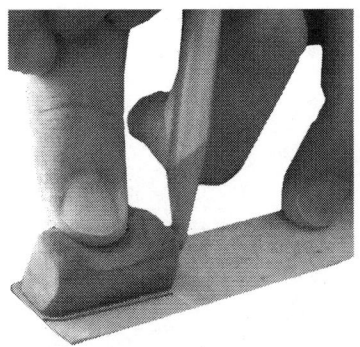
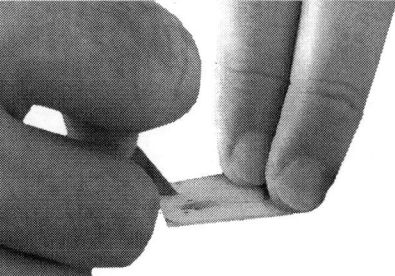
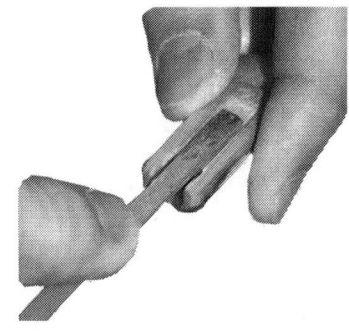

b. Use the exacting knife to cut the hobby wood to cover the bird's underside.

c. Carefully cut a 1/4-inch wide strip out of the middle of the hobby piece, starting at what will be the fetish's notched end to about 1/4-inch from the solid opposite end.

d. Glue the strip of wood to the fetish and allow to dry.

5. Use a flat needle file and fine-grade sandpaper to remove remnants and smooth and the channel.

6. Using leather strings, leather strip, twine, or other material, secure the fetish to the flute.

7. Test for proper airflow by blowing through the mouthpiece.

8. If the flute sounds too airy, decrease the channel depth by small increments, testing frequently until the desired sound is achieved.

9. If notes are not clear, examine the channel and how the fetish sits upon the flute. Determine if air leaks exist around base or if the channel depth requires adjustment to direct air properly across the labium.

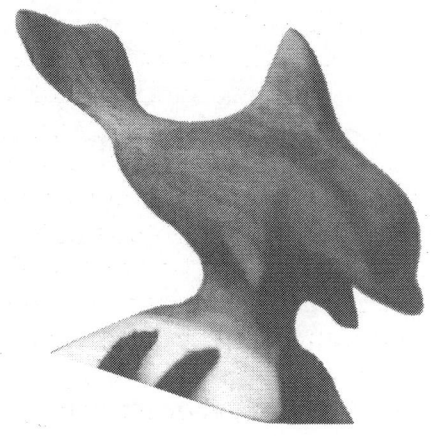

Chapter Eight

The Modern Native American Flute

The modern, two-chamber Native American flute has a primary advantage over instruments like the Anasazi flute, quena, shakuhachi, and other rim-blown and transverse flutes—being a whistle makes it a lot easier to play. For crafters, however, making the two-chamber flute is a more involved and time-consuming process than making the ancient version.

As the Native American flute's popularity surged in the 1980s and 1990s, a debate surfaced over distinguishing the flute into two types, the Plains flute and Woodlands flute. Some crafters and players argue that one is more authentic than the other, but when defining what makes one different from or superior to the other, lines blur. The primary difference is the air channel—specifically, whether it's carved into the body of the flute, created by a spacer, or carved into the base of the bird. Depending on the player, maker, or historian, other factors complicate the issue.

Most agree that Woodlands flutes incorporate the air channel in the flute barrel, carved between the air chamber hole and sound hole. A Plains flute can incorporate the channel in either the flute body or bird underside. Some insist that Woodlands flutes utilize a blunted labium edge and Plains flutes a sharpened edge. Woodlands flutes are supposedly crafted with a larger bore, although bore size is usually chosen to best render a specific key or to increase or decrease finger hole proximity. Another factor can be the mouthpiece. If it's tapered to fit between the lips, some claim it's a Plains flute. If it's blunted to fit against the mouth, it's purportedly a Woodlands flute. For some, the crafting method rather than design defines the type of flute. A Woodlands flute, for example, should have holes burned into it with a heated metal rod or embers on the end of burning stick. Sound, air, and finger holes of Plains flutes, however, can be either drilled or burned.

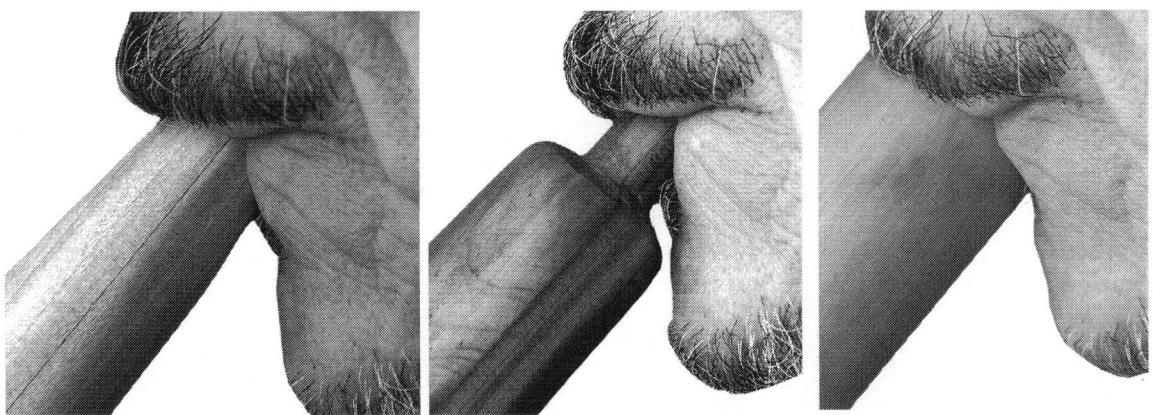

Examples of mouthpieces include, a slightly tapered, blunted mouthpiece, a nipple mouthpiece, and an open-end mouthpiece, usually utilized with bamboo and PVC flutes.

Confusion arises when characteristics of one type of flute are mixed with characteristics of the other, leaving only the labium—blunt or sharp—as the defining aspect. Even then, disagreement persists. Perhaps the best solution is to call both what they are—Native American flutes—and leave the subjective classification to those who'd rather debate details than create music.

Over the centuries, the number of finger holes has varied on native flutes. The modern Native American flute has been standardized to have either six holes or five holes. On 5-hole flutes, the space that would be the fourth finger hole on a 6-hole flute is left closed. Players who prefer the 5-hole flute, as mentioned earlier, maintain that the fourth hole on a 6-hole flute is superfluous, that all notes produced by the 6-hole flute can be achieved on the 5-hole flute. The fingering required to achieve the same notes, however, is more complex than fingering on the 6-hole flute.

Each crafter's technique is in some way unique, despite similarities between all crafters. Some prefer traditional authenticity and do everything by hand with the simplest of tools, from splitting and hollowing wood with knives and gouges (which were the "modern" tools used by crafters at one time), to shaping and finishing with specialty carving knives or homemade implements. Crafters at the opposite end of the spectrum relish modern tools and techniques, utilizing routers and lathes to create perfectly crafted bores and rounded flutes that vastly surpass the ability of traditional hand tools. Others skip the challenges and frustrations of wood altogether by using bamboo or PVC pipe. Choice, therefore, comes down to individual desire and ability.

External conditions can affect the crafting process. Many crafters maintain that tuning a flute must be accomplished at a specific ambient temperature, around 70° Fahrenheit, believing that a median temperature during crafting will ensure the flute plays close to key in varying temperatures. Problems will still arise, though, due to the player's breath which warms the flute, causing notes to sharpen no matter the temperature during crafting and tuning. For this reason, I tune flutes slightly flat to allow the player's breath to bring a flute more into tune as it warms.

Whether a note plays flat or sharp is also affected by the force of breath. The stronger the air stream, the sharper the note; the slower, the flatter. The force needed to produce the flute's higher notes is stronger than needed for the fundamental and lower notes. When tuning, maintain a steady pressure and airstream.

If you finish the flute with paint or lacquer, it's okay to spray the nest and fetish, including the channel, but don't over-spray. Over-spraying may clog the channel and air and sound holes or cause the nest to become lumpy, which can create air turbulence that will affect note production.

Finally, if you're a purist, you may want to craft a flute utilizing the traditional method that requires only the crafter's body for measurements. Although strictly a solo instrument, a traditionally crafted flute offers a unique crafting and musical experience, an instrument that no other crafter can duplicate. The traditional crafting method is detailed following instructions for crafting the modern native flute.

General Measurements

When it comes to crafting the native flute, everything is subject to adjustment. Consider the following measurements and methods as general guidelines. By experimentation, you may find that the measurements determined through the following instructions work best for your crafting needs, or you may find variations serve you better.

1. Sound hole: 1/4-inch square

2. Labium/air split: 45-degree angle, 1/16-inch thick blunt

3. Channel: 1/16-inch deep, 1/4-inch wide

4. Wall thickness of flute: 5/16-inch

5. For finger hole placement, use the following percentages and formula:

   Sound Chamber Length (from sound hole midpoint to foot) x Percentage = Hole Placement

   - hole 1, 64.5 percent from labium hole
   - hole 2, 58 percent
   - hole 3, 51 percent
   - hole 4, 44 percent (omit on 5-hole flutes)
   - hole 5, 38 percent
   - hole 6, 31 percent

Modern Native American Flute Tuning Scale

Six-Hole Tuning Guide

Fundamental/ Key	Hole 1	Hole 2	Hole 3	Hole 4	Hole 5	Hole 6
F#	A	B	C#	Eb	F	G
G	Bb	C	D	E	F#	G#
G#	B	C#	Eb	F	G	A
A	C	D	E	F#	G#	A#
Bb	C#	Eb	F	G	A	B
B	D	E	F#	G#	Bb	C
C	Eb	F	G	A	B	C#
C#	E	F#	G#	Bb	C	D
D	F	G	A	B	C#	Eb
Eb	F#	G#	Bb	C	D	F
E	G	A	B	C#	Eb	F#
F	G#	Bb	C	D	F	G

(Handwritten margin notes: 21 1/4, 18 1/8, 15", 14 1/4, low 22 1/4, 21 1/2, 19 5/8)

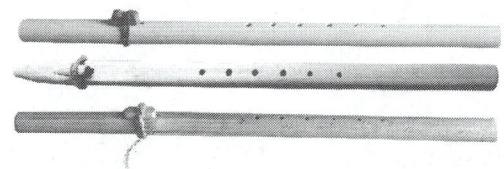

Five-Hole Tuning Guide

Fundamental/ Key	Hole 1	Hole 2	Hole 3	Hole 4	Hole 5
F#	A	B	C#	E	F#
G	Bb	C	D	F	G
G#	B	C#	Eb	F#	G#
A	C	D	E	G	A
Bb	C#	Eb	F	G#	Bb
B	D	E	F#	A	B
C	Eb	F	G	Bb	C
C#	E	F#	G#	B	C#
D	F	G	A	C	D
Eb	F#	G#	Bb	C#	Eb
E	G	A	B	D	F
F	G#	Bb	C	Eb	F#

Craft the Wood Flute

Refer to Chapter Seven for instructions on crafting the bird/fetish. Then proceed with the instructions for crafting the flute.

Materials

- 1/2 x 4 x 24-inch hobby board, available in pine, poplar, oak, and other woods, depending on store stock, or 1/2 x 4 x 24-inch aromatic cedar planks, usually a mail-order item (I utilize naturally downed wood on many projects and hobby board from sustained sources to speed the process on others.)
- 2 x 2 x 1-inch pine or cedar wood (basic fetish; refer to fetish instructions in Chapter Seven)
- leather, twine, or other string to secure bird to flute
- cork or wood dowel to match channel bore, approximately 1/2-inch long
- carpenter's glue
- fine, medium, coarse sandpaper

- finishing oil (linseed, tung oil, etc.)
- spray lacquer or paint (optional)

Tools

- electronic chromatic tuner (tuning applications for computers and smartphones provide an excellent alternative to a stand-alone tuner)
- electric sander (optional)
- tape measure
- small handsaw or hacksaw
- electric table saw
- straightedge 24 inches or longer
- wood clamps (C-clamps, bar clamps, etc.), at least four but number will depend on flute length
- 3-inch trimming hand plane
- electric router
- router table
- 3/4-inch core box router bit
- rotary tool and/or high-speed drill
- 1/8-inch drill bit to fit drill and rotary tool
- flat and rounded needle files, no wider than 1/4-inch
- homemade sanding rod

Homemade Sanding Rod

1. Cut a slit the width of the sanding paper in one end of the dowel.
2. Insert one end of the sandpaper.
3. Wrap the sheet of sandpaper around the dowel, rough side out.
4. To better secure the paper, apply glue to the underside of the final layer.
5. Secure by wrapping with a rubber band to ensure the exterior layer's underside maintains contact with the interior layer.
6. Allow to dry before use.

Router Setup

1. Attach the router to the router table according to manufacturer instructions.

 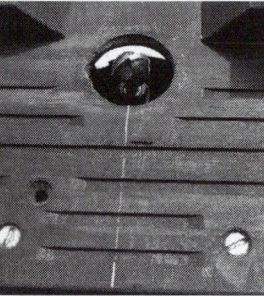

2. Mark the wood to be routed for a bit height of 3/8-inch.

3. Place the wood on the router table against the router bit.

4. Adjust the router bit up or down so that the point on top rests at the mark on the wood.

5. Mark from the side midpoint of the router bit to the midpoint of the table's side to act as a guide point when routing

6. Set the router table guide to ensure at least 1/4-inch of wood between the table guide and channel.

Craft the Flute

Photographs of the crafting process follow these instructions.

1. Mark the wood two inches from the mouthpiece end as the stopping point for channel routing.

2. Rout the first half from the foot to the marked point. Switch off the router, allow router to stop completely. Remove wood.

3. Rout the second half. If using hobby board, flip the board over to rout the second channel.

4. If crafting with hobby board, rip the plank lengthwise with a table saw or handsaw to separate channels, making sure at least 1/4-inch wall remains between channel walls and cut.

5. Wrap fine grade sandpaper around a dowel for more uniform sanding. Sand the channel halves. Sand *only* the interior and not the top of the channels where the halves will be joined.

6. Insert a plug approximately 1-1/5 to 2 inches from mouthpiece end of channel. A plug cut from a dowel the same diameter as the channel or a ⸻k will suffice. I prefer cork ⸻xibility.

⸻ hole on both
⸻ Shaping
⸻r as-

⸻

⸻ney
bar-

anassl

☐

49.5
41,58
38.61
35.64
29.70
27.225
24.255

rel.

10. Clamp the flute and allow to dry at least 24 hours.

11. Drill the mouthpiece hole to the air channel.

12. Craft the fetish if you have not already done so. Refer to instructions in Chapter Seven.

14 ¼

13. Shape the labium and air holes into approximately 1/4-inch squares, making certain they are shaped inline.

14. File the sound hole's foot underside at roughly a 45-degree angle to form a 1/16-inch blunt edge.

15. Test the flute for sound, fine-adjusting the fetish, labium, and air hole to obtain the desired sound. If the sound is too airy, reduce channel depth. If airflow is restricted, increase channel depth. Seat the fetish properly over the air and labium holes. If no note sounds, check the labium for uniformity, dust, fragments, etc.

16. Use the tuner to determine the fundamental note. Shorten the barrel incrementally, 1/4-inch each time, to raise the fundamental to pitch.

17. With a straightedge, draw a line from the middle of the sound hole to the flute's foot as a guide for uniform placement of finger holes.

18. Calculate and mark finger holes using the following formula and percentages.

Sound Chamber Length (from sound hole to foot) x Percentage = Hole Placement

- hole 1, 64.5 percent from labium hole
- hole 2, 58 percent
- hole 3, 51 percent
- hole 4, 44 percent *
- hole 5, 38 percent
- hole 6, 31 percent
  * For a 5-hole flute, do not drill hole 4. Refer to tuning charts to see how the fourth hole omission affects the tuning of holes five and six. Placement percentages for holes 5 and 6 are unaffected.

19. Drill hole 1 no larger than 1/8-inch. Determine the hole's pitch. It should be lower than desired.

20. With a half-round or round needle file, raise the pitch to target note by enlarging the hole incrementally toward the sides and labium, testing frequently until the desired pitch is attained.

21. Proceed to the remaining holes, drilling and tuning each to desired pitch before proceeding to the next.

22. With the small hand planer, rough-shape the wood into a conventional flute barrel. Draw a guide circle the thickness desired—1/8-inch to

1/4-inch—around the tube bore. Plane the foot end to desired thickness.

23. Using the planed foot section as a guide, plane the flute to the fetish and nest area, but leave nest flat.

24. Depending on preference, leave the mouthpiece end blunt or taper the barrel to form the mouthpiece.

25. Either by hand or with an electric sander, fine shape the barrel, beginning with coarse paper, followed by medium and fine grades.

26. Fine-sand finger holes to remove fragments. Do not enlarge the holes any further af-

ter tuning to correct pitch.

27. Fine-sand both the interior and exterior of the flute. Use the homemade sanding rod for interior.

28. Apply pre-finish, if desired, such as stain or oil. Allow to dry 24 hours before proceeding to final steps.

29. With a clean cloth, remove dust from the interior and exterior.

30. Finish the flute as desired. I prefer spray lacquer, applying it first to the barrel interior and then exterior after the interior's dried. Allow final coat to dry for at least 24 hours.

Craft the Wood Flute Illustrated

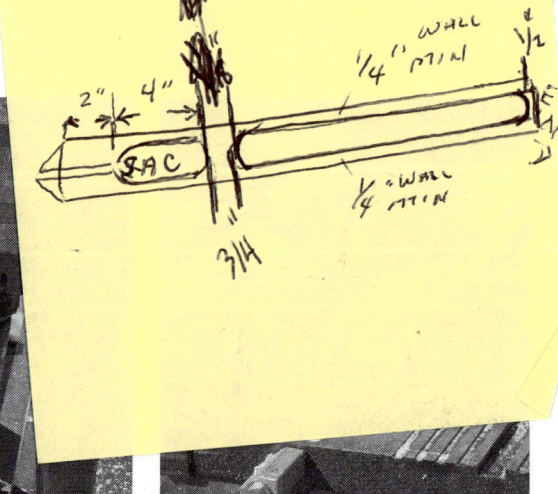

Rout the first channel.

Flip the board to rout second channel.

Rip the board to separate the channels.

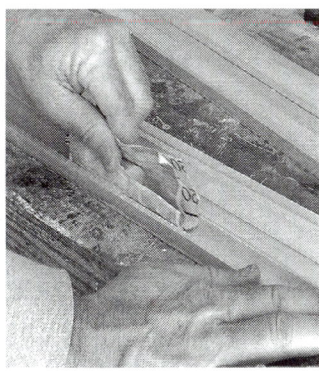
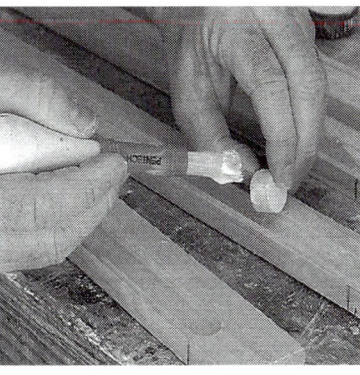
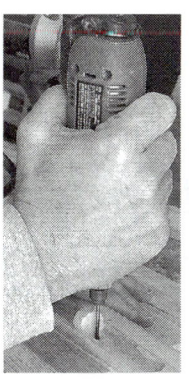

Sand the interior of the channels.

Apply glue to the air plug and place it into one channel.

Drill the air and sound holes.

Clean channels with an oil-damp cloth.

Apply glue to contact points of both channels.

Assemble the two halves to form the bore.

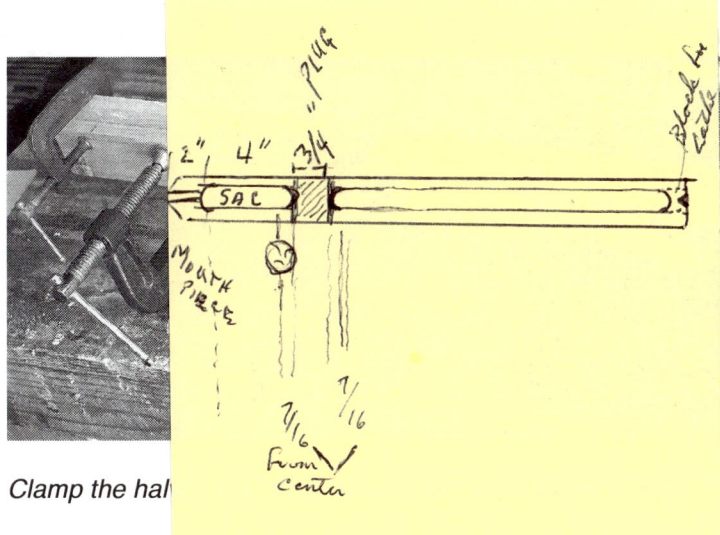

Clamp the hal

Drill the mouth-piece hole.

Shape the air and sound holes.

Determine the fundamental note.

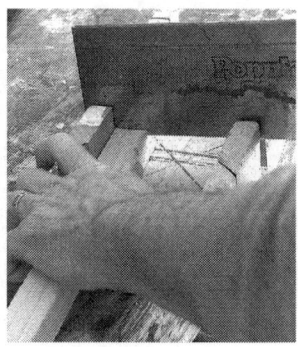

Shorten the barrel length to raise pitch to desired fundamental.

Calculate and mark finger-hole positions.

Drill the first finger hole with 1/8-inch bit. Using needle files, enlarge it incrementally to the correct pitch an then proceed to each successive hole.

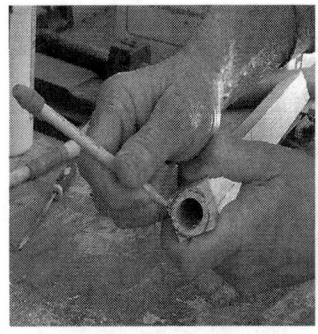

Mark to plane.

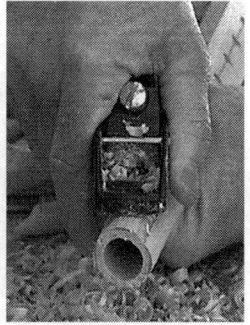

Rough plane the ends, then the middle.

Fine shape and sand the flute.

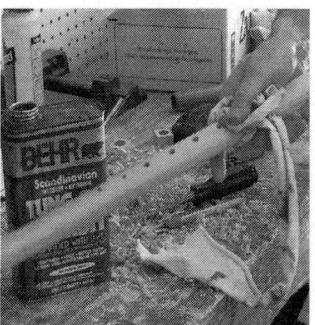

Clean flute exterior with oil-damp rag.

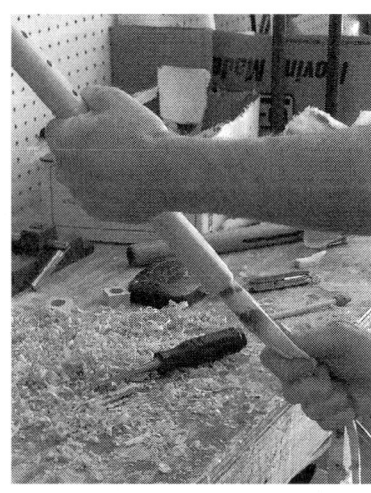 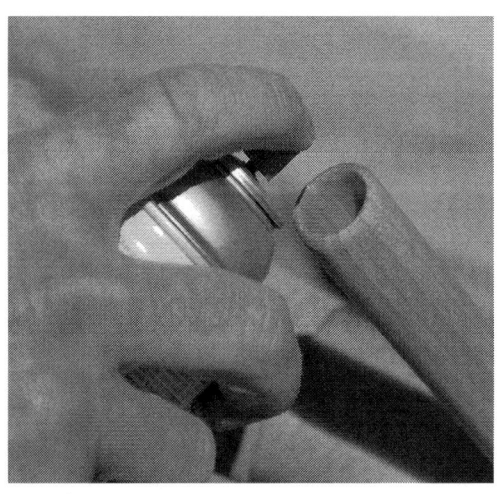 

With oil-damp rag attached to a dowel, clean the flute barrel.

If desired and to better protect from humidity fluctuations, spray the barrel interior with lacquer.

Finish the exterior with lacquer or paint. Allow at least 24 hours to dry.

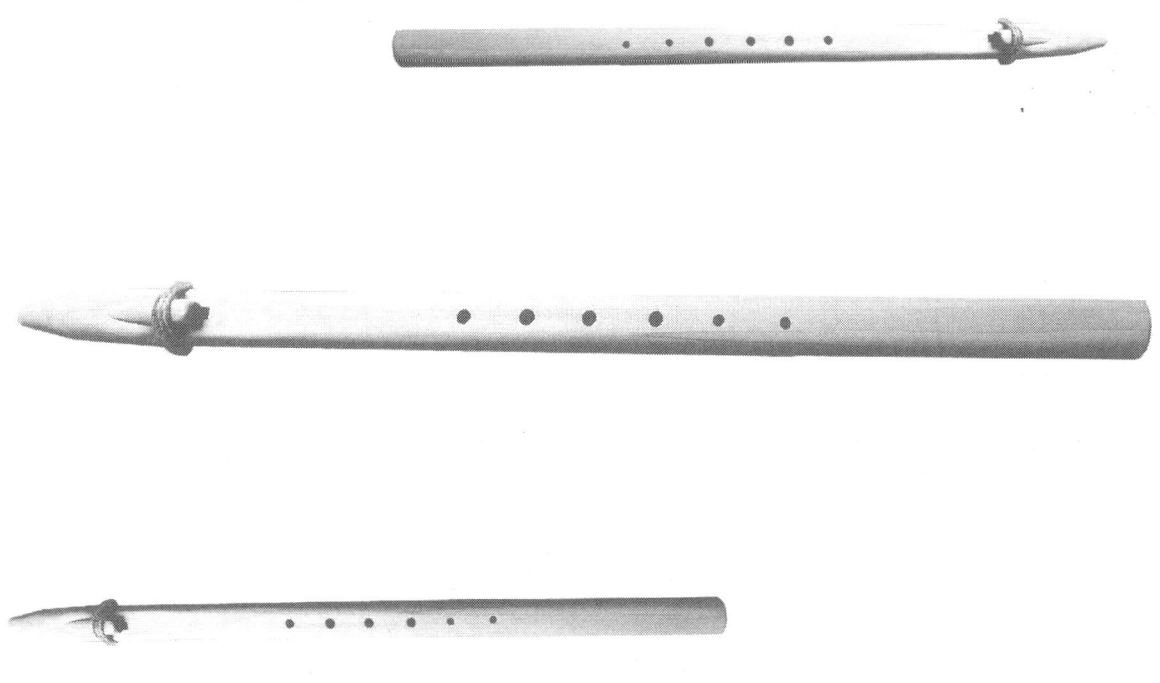

Craft the Bamboo Flute

Materials

- 24-inch length of bamboo, 3/4-inch bore or larger, with 4 inches on one side of node for slow air chamber and 20 inches on opposite side of node
- 2 x 2 x 1-inch pine or cedar wood for fetish (please refer to instructions in Chapter Seven)
- leather, twine, or other string to secure bird to flute
- carpenter's glue
- fine, medium, coarse sandpaper
- spray lacquer (optional)
- waxed string such as hemp for binding (optional)

Tools

- electronic chromatic tuner (tuning applications for computers and smartphones provide an excellent alternative to a stand-alone tuner)
- electric sander (optional)
- tape measure
- small handsaw or hacksaw
- straightedge at least 24 inches long
- rotary tool (a standard drill's speed is too slow and can easily split bamboo, rendering it useless)
- 1/8-inch rotary tool drill bit
- standard drill
- extra-long drill bit with approximate diameter of bamboo bore

- flat and rounded needle files, no wider than 1/4-inch
- homemade sanding rod
- sanding block (a homemade sanding block consists of a 1 x 2 x 3-inch piece of wood wrapped with sandpaper)

Craft the Flute

Photographs of the crafting process follow these instructions.

1. Cut the mouthpiece end to a length of 3 to 4 inches from the plug node.

2. Cut the sound chamber side at least 18 inches long.

3. Remove all interior nodes *except* the node between the air and sound chambers, with an extra-long drill bit the approximate size of the bamboo bore.

4. Use the homemade sanding rod to smooth the bore where nodes have been removed.

5. (optional) With all nodes except the blocking node removed, bake the bamboo at 275 degrees for approximately 20-30 minutes. The bamboo's oils will provide a natural finish to the wood similar to lacquer. Drilling and sanding will remove sections of this finish that can be covered by lacquer or other desired finishing product.

6. With the sanding block, sand the barrel exterior air plug

node at least 1/2-inch on each side to form a flat, rectangular nest for the bird.

7. Use the rotary tool with a 1/8-inch drill bit to drill the air hole on the mouthpiece side of the node and the air hole on the sound chamber side of the node. The air and sound holes should be next to the node, about 1/2- to 3/4-inch apart.

8. Shape the air and sound holes into 1/4-inch squares, making certain the holes are shaped inline.

9. File the splitting edge (foot underside of sound hole) at a 45-degree angle to a 1/16-inch thick blunt edge.

10. Using the instructions in Chapter Seven, craft the bird.

11. Secure the bird and adjust the fetish and/or sound hole to obtain desired sound. If the sound is too airy, reduce the channel depth. If airflow is restricted, increase channel depth. Make sure the fetish is seated properly over the air hole and at the mouthpiece edge of the sound hole. If no note sounds, check the channel and labium for uniformity and anomalies. You may have to experiment to attain the sound desired.

12. With the tuner, determine the fundamental of the current length. Shorten the barrel by 1/4- to 1/2-inch with each cut until desired pitch is reached.

13. With a straightedge, draw a line from middle of the blowing edge to the flute's foot end to ensure uniform finger hole placement.

14. Bore diameter will vary between different pieces of bamboo. It's unlikely you'll find a bore that is exactly 3/4-inch diameter. Therefore, utilize the following formula and percentages to determine finger-hole placement:

Sound Chamber Length (from sound hole to foot) x Percentage = Hole Placement

- hole 1, 64.5 percent from sound hole midpoint
- hole 2, 58 percent
- hole 3, 51 percent
- hole 4, 44 percent*
- hole 5, 38 percent
- hole 6, 31 percent

For a 5-hole flute, do not drill the number 4 hole. Refer to tuning charts to see how the fourth hole omission affects the tuning of holes five and six. Placement percentages for holes remain the same as those of the 6-hole flute.

15. Along the guideline, mark finger hole placement as calculated.

16. Use a high-speed rotary tool to drill holes. A conventional drill can easily split bamboo, rendering it useless.

17. Drill hole 1 no larger than 1/8-inch. Determine its pitch.

18. With a half-round or round needle file, raise the pitch by enlarging the hole incrementally, primarily toward the sides and sound hole, testing frequently to reach the desired pitch.

19. Proceed to the remaining holes, bringing each to desired pitch before proceeding to the next.

20. Fine-sand each hole to remove fragments, careful not to enlarge holes any further after attaining correct pitch.

21. Fine-sand both interior and exterior of the flute. Use the homemade sanding rod for the interior.

22. If the bamboo has not been baked or has been sanded, apply an oil finish, such as tung or linseed oil, allowing 24 hours to dry before proceeding to the final step.

23. With a clean cloth, remove dust from the interior and exterior. Finish the flute with paint or lacquer. I prefer spray lacquer, available in assorted colors, including clear and black, applying it first to the interior barrel, then exterior. Apply a second coat after the first has dried at least 45 minutes. Do not over-spray to avoid runs and a lumpy finish. Allow the final coat to dry for at least 24 hours.

24. Bind the flute if desired (see Chapter Four).

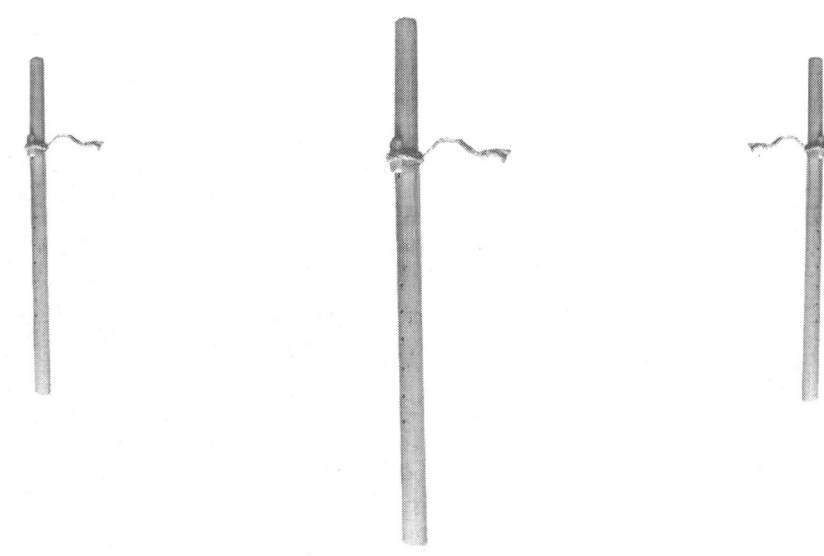

Craft the Bamboo Flute Illustrated

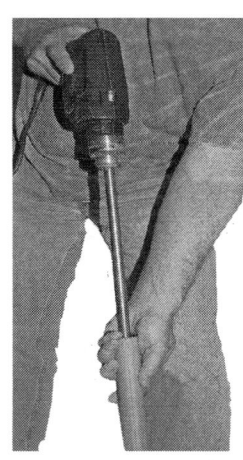

Bake the bamboo for 20-25 minutes at 275°F.   Drill out nodes.

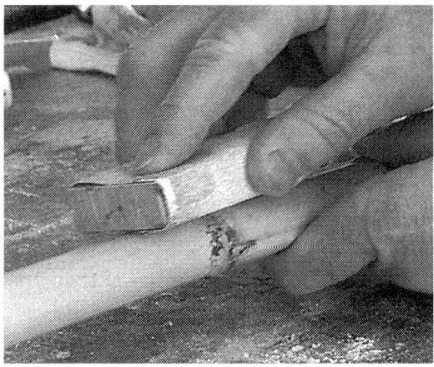

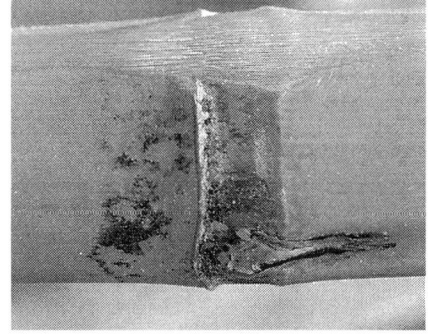

Flatten the node between chambers to create nest.

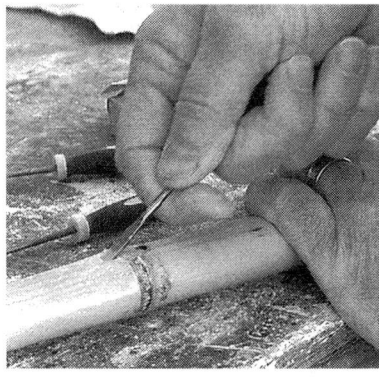

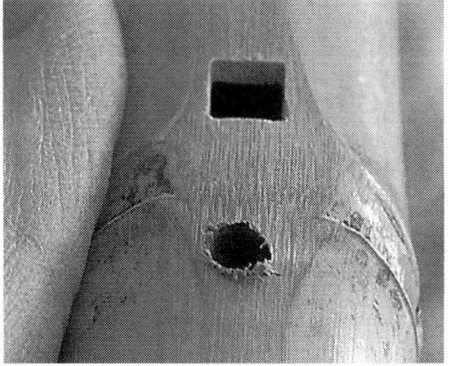

Drill and shape air and sound holes.

Shape sound hole foot underside to blunt air splitting edge.

Shorten incrementally to reach desired fundamental note.

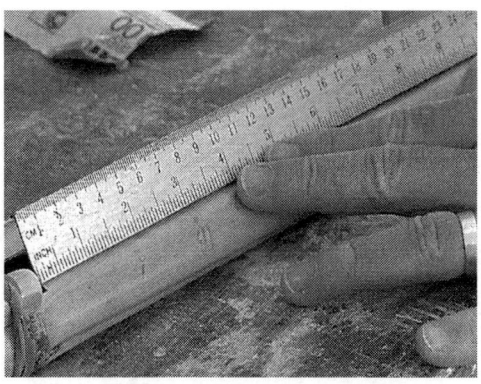

Calculate and mark finger-hole placement.

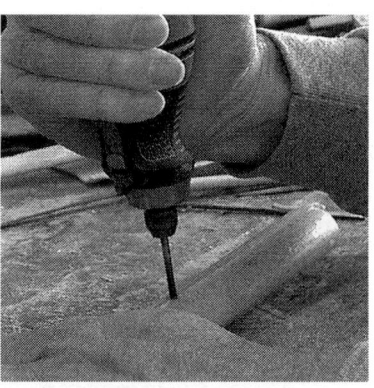

Drill finger holes one by one, no more than 1/8-inch.

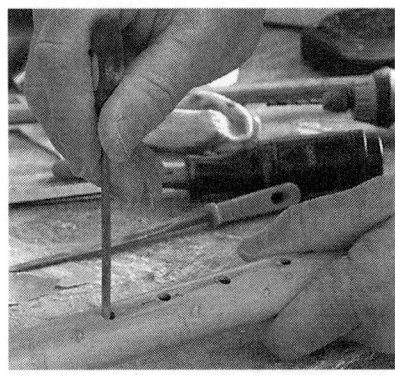

Enlarge incrementally with a rounded needle file, testing the note often.

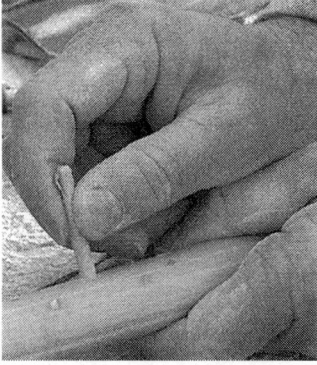

Use fine-grade sandpaper to remove remnants. Do not enlarge further after achieving target note.

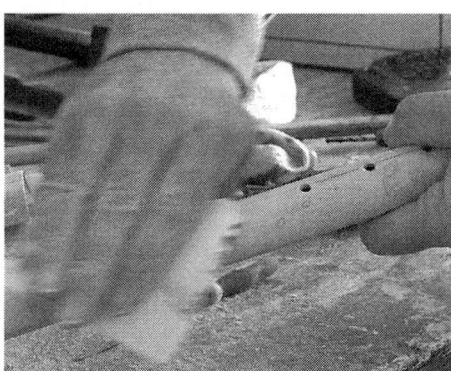

Fine-sand exterior and interior.

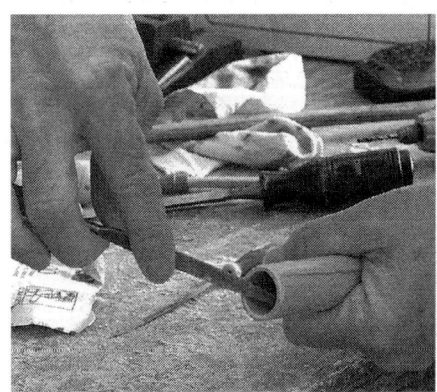

Soften edges in the foot and mouthpiece ends by using a rounded needle file.

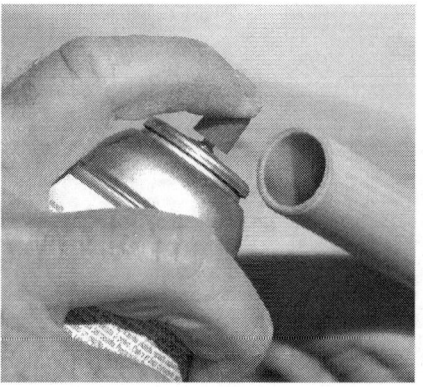

To protect from breath moisture, finish the interior barrel with spray lacquer.

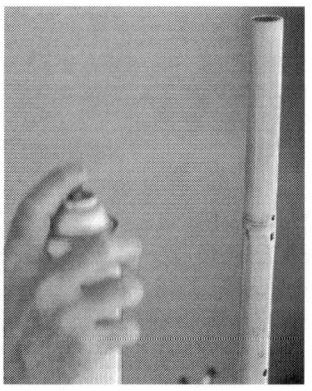

To protect and provide an attractive appearance, finish with spray lacquer.

Craft the PVC Flute

Materials

- 24-inch length PVC pipe, 3/4- to 1-inch diameter
- for fetish, either 2 x 2 x 1-inch wood or PVC pipe connector (refer to Chapter Seven)
- leather, twine, or other string to secure wood bird to flute
- 1-inch long cork or wood dowel, PVC bore diameter
- fine, medium, coarse sandpaper
- spray lacquer (optional)
- cleanser
- fine grade steel wool

Tools

- electronic chromatic tuner (tuning applications for computers and smartphones provide an excellent alternative to a stand-alone tuner)
- handsaw or hacksaw
- tape measure
- straightedge at least two-feet long
- rotary tool
- 1/8-inch rotary tool drill bit
- 1/4-inch wide flat and rounded needle files
- standard flat wood file (optional)
- sanding block (a homemade sanding block consists of a 1 x 2 x 3-inch piece of wood wrapped with sandpaper)
- sanding rod

Craft the Flute

Photographs of the crafting process follow these instructions.

1. Cut a 24-inch length of 3/4-inch or 1-inch interior diameter PVC pipe.

2. 3 to 4 inches from one end (this will be the mouthpiece end), drill a 1/8-inch air hole.

3. 1/2-inch to 3/4-inch from the air hole toward the foot end of the flute, drill the sound hole in line with the air hole.

4. Use the sanding block or wood file to flatten the barrel between the sound and air holes from 1/4-inch beyond each hole. Flatten only enough to form the rectangular nest, about 3/16-inch wide.

5. Cut the cork or dowel to a length that fits between the two holes, insert it into the mouthpiece end, and, using a dowel or other instrument that will fit into the interior, push the plug into place between the air and sound holes.

6. Shape the sound and air holes into 1/4-inch squares, making certain the holes are inline. The air hole can be round if preferred.

7. File the air hole's foot under-

side to roughly a 45-degree angle, creating a labium with an approximate 1/16-inch thick blunt edge.

8. Secure the fetish on the nest. Make sure the fetish is seated properly over the air and labium holes.

9. Test the flute for sound and make adjustments as needed. If no note is produced, check the sound hole for uniformity and anomalies. If the sound is too airy, reduce the channel depth. If airflow is restricted, increase the depth. You may have to experiment.

10. Bring the fundamental/key note to desired pitch by shortening the flute's foot end incrementally, cutting no more than 1/4-inch off at a time, testing the note after each cut.

11. Using a straightedge, draw a line from the middle of the sound hole to the foot end as a guide for uniform placement of finger holes.

12. Use the following formula and percentages to determine finger hole placement:

Sound Chamber Length

(from sound hole to foot) x Percentage = Hole Placement

- hole 1, 64.5 percent from labium hole
- hole 2, 58 percent
- hole 3, 51 percent
- hole 4, 44 percent*
- hole 5, 38 percent
- hole 6, 31 percent

For a 5-hole flute, do not drill the number four hole. Refer to tuning charts to see how the fourth hole omission affects the tuning of holes five and six. Placement percentages remain the same.

13. Enlarge each hole incrementally to desired pitch before proceeding to the next hole.

14. After completing the finger holes, remove PVC remnants from the barrel interior by using the sanding rod.

15. With fine grade steel wool and cleanser, remove factory-applied lettering from the flute's exterior.

16. If desired, apply a coat of lacquer to the barrel interior and exterior and allow to dry 24 hours.

Craft the PVC Flute Illustrated

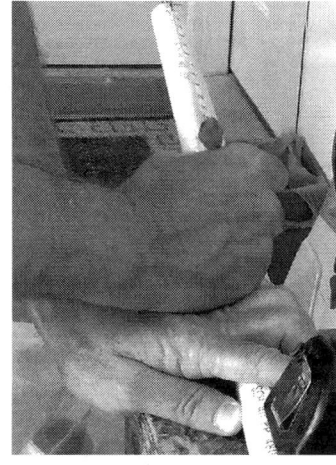

Measure a 24-inch length of PVC 3/4-inch diameter pipe.

With a fine-tooth saw, cut the length of pipe.

Drill the 1/8-inch air hole 3 to 4 inches from desired mouthpiece end. Drill sound hole inline 1/2-inch to 3/4-inch from first hole toward the foot.

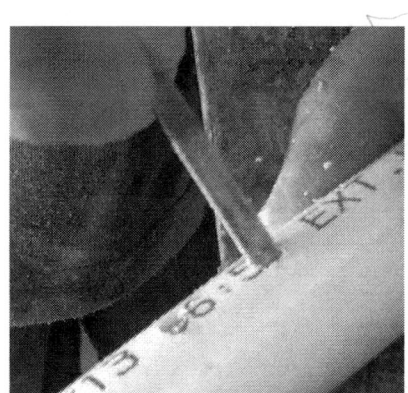

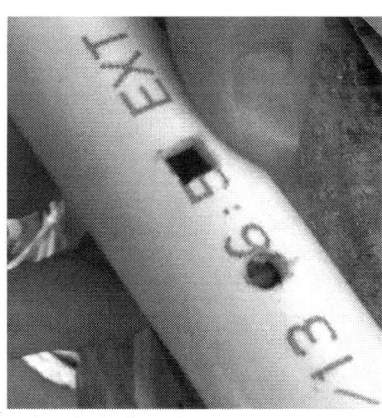

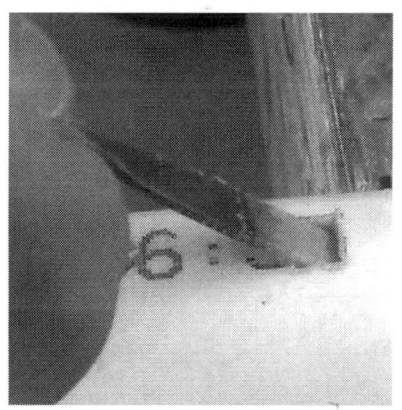

Shape inline the air and sound holes to 1/4-inch square.

The air hole can be round or square as desired.

Shape sound hole's foot underside at 45-degree angle to form 1/16-inch blunt edge.

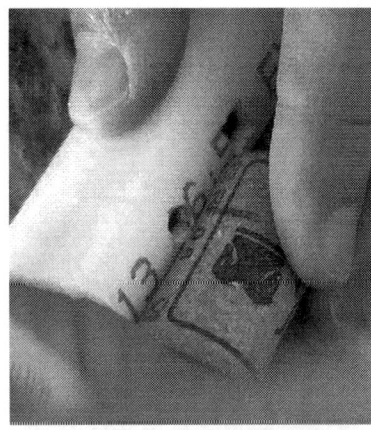

Measure cork or dowel for plug between air and sound holes.

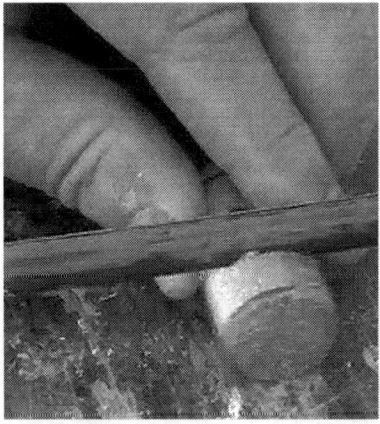

Cut cork or dowel.

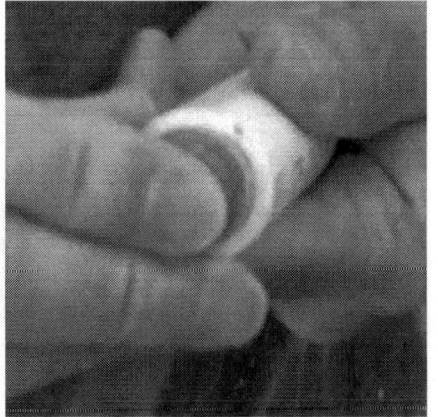

Insert cork or dowel into mouthpiece end.

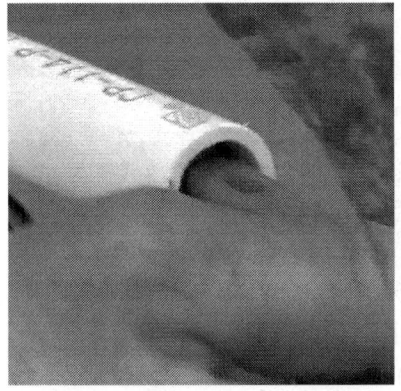

With blunt instrument, move the plug into place between air and sound holes.

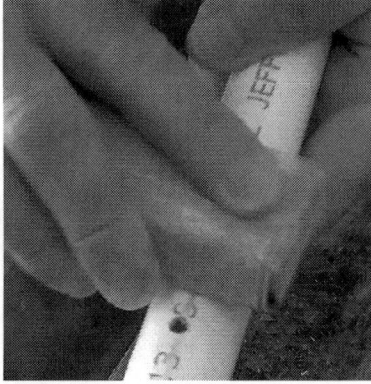

Flatten the nest area.

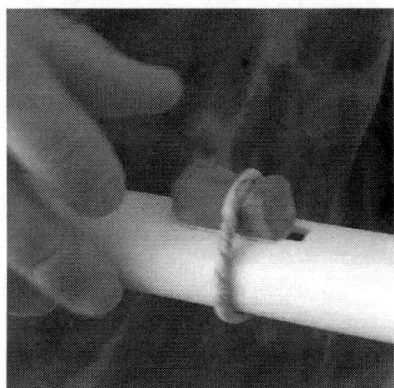

Secure the fetish and determine the fundamental note.

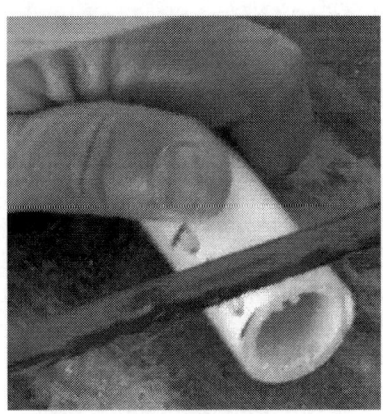

Shorten the pipe by increments to reach desired fundamental.

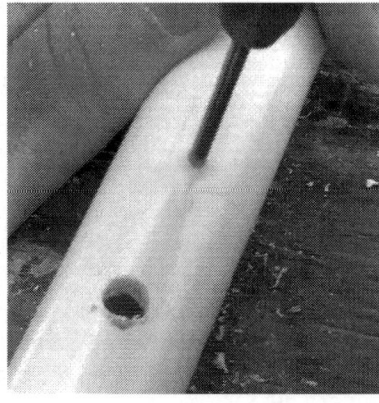

Calculate, mark, and drill the finger holes, tuning each before proceeding to the next.

Remove remnants with fine sandpaper. Do not enlarge hole after reaching desired note.

Craft the Traditional Flute

Previous instructions apply strictly to crafting the modern Native American flute tuned to the pentatonic scale, enabling the flute to accompany other instruments. Traditional Native American flutes were solo instruments, accompanied at most by a drum or voice. Traditional flutes were unique to themselves and to the maker. If crafting an instrument that only you can make is appealing, then read on. These instructions apply to PVC, wood, and bamboo construction. Please refer to the illustration below for measuring clarification.

Materials

- 1/2 x 4 x 24-inch hobby board, 1/2 x 4 x 24-inch aromatic cedar planks, or 24-inch length of 3/4-inch diameter bamboo or PVC pipe
- 2 x 2 x 1-inch wood or appropriate size PVC connector for bird (see Chapter Seven)
- leather, twine, or other string to secure bird to flute
- 1/2-inch length cork or wood dowel to match channel bore

- carpenter's glue
- fine, medium, coarse sandpaper
- finishing oil (linseed, tung oil, etc.)
- spray lacquer (optional)

Tools

- electric router for wood
- electric sander (optional)
- tape measure
- small handsaw or hacksaw
- power table saw for wood
- straightedge 24 inches or longer
- at least four wood clamps for wood flute
- 3-inch trimming hand plane for wood flute
- power router for wood flute
- router table for wood flute
- 3/4-inch core box router bit for wood flute
- rotary tool
- high-speed drill
- 1/8-inch drill bit
- long drill bit for bamboo
- 1/4-inch flat and rounded needle files
- sanding rod

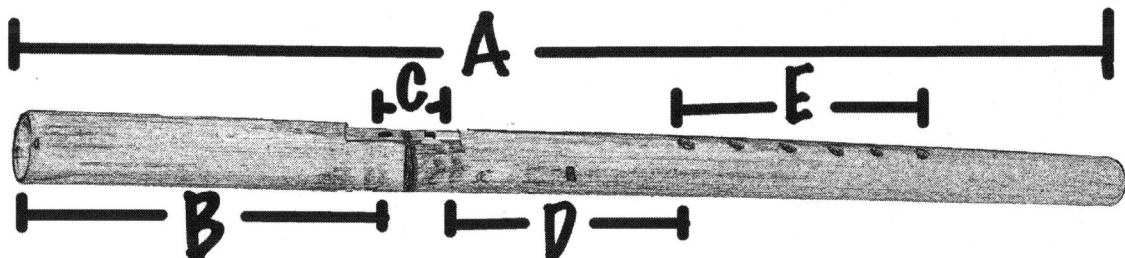

A: Length from crafter's elbow to outstretched fingertips.
B and D: Width of crafter's hand.
C and E: Width of crafter's thumb.

Craft the Flute

1. For wood, rout two halves at least 24 inches in length end-to-end.

2. Do not insert a plug at this point. Assemble the two halves. A plug will be inserted when air and sound hole placement is determined.

3. For all materials, measure from elbow to outstretched fingertips to determine flute length and cut to length.

4. Determine placement of the air hole by the width of the maker's hand from the flute's mouthpiece end.

5. Drill and shape the air hole.

6. Determine placement of the sound hole by the width of the maker's thumb from the foot side of the air hole to the mouthpiece side of the sound hole.

7. Drill and shape the sound hole.

8. Measure and cut dowel or cork to fit between air and sound holes.

9. Insert dowel or cork. Slide it between the sound and air holes.

10. Determine placement of the sixth finger hole (the one closest to the sound hole) by the width of the maker's hand from the foot side of the sound hole to the finger hole.

11. Drill hole.

12. Determine the placement of the remaining finger holes by the width of the maker's thumb.

13. Drill each hole.

14. Enlarge each hole to a pitch that is pleasing and complementary to the pitches/notes of the preceding holes.

15. Shape the flute if wooden.

16. Remove remnants from the interior barrel with the sanding rod.

17. Remove remnants from the air hole, sound hole, and finger holes with fine-grade sandpaper.

18. From coarse to fine, sand the flute interior and exterior if bamboo or wood.

19. For PVC, use fine-grade steel wool and cleanser to clean exterior and interior.

20. For wood and bamboo, finish with oil, lacquer, or paint as desired. Finish PVC with paint as desired.

Chapter Nine

The Drone

The Native American double or triple flute, or drone, is sometimes cited as a modern invention, an experimentation that produced a pleasant result, but drone flutes have been around for quite sometime, primarily in Mesoamerican cultures such as the Aztec and Mayan. In all cultures worldwide, music has been and remains associated with every aspect of life, from celebration to mourning, peace to war, love to hatred. Historians believe that a primary function of the Native American flute was spiritual, to honor and thank gods for blessings in daily life and to enhance spiritual requests.

In Mesoamerican cultures, a variety of wind instruments, from true, end-blown flutes to whistles and ocarinas, were utilized in both spiritual and everyday activities. Images of respected animals commonly adorned most instruments, while many ocarinas were crafted fully in the images of birds, snakes, coyotes and other animals, and insects.

Mesoamerican flutes usually had two to five holes and ranged in length from four inches to more than twelve inches. Unlike the North American Native American flute, Mesoamerican flutes were made usually of clay, many similar in shape to modern trumpets. Surviving examples of the clay flutes are often double chambered like the wooden flute of North American cultures. Drone flute artifacts from the El Salvador region date from at least 1250 BCE. Triple-barrel flutes have also been found, suggesting Mesoamerican flute crafters may have possessed a more vibrant curiosity for musical experimentation than their northern counterparts

Drone flutes enable a flautist to play a melody on one barrel while a single accompanying note drones from the second barrel. Most of the drone artifact flutes uncovered to date do not conform to any standard in tuning, instead producing varied scales and odd acoustical effects that historians believe were important in various rituals, based on era mural art depicting flutes in ceremonial use.

The modern Native American drone flute is available in various forms, including the shotgun type, incorporating both barrels as part of a single unit; two or more separate flutes glued or strapped together side-by-side; and two or three flutes connected by a bridge to form a V or W configuration.

The primary material for modern drone flutes is wood, bamboo, or PVC, while clay flutes tend to be a specialty pursued by a minority of makers. Unlike the ancient drone flutes, today's drones are usually tuned to the pentatonic scale, with six finger holes on one barrel and none on the drone barrel, which most commonly delivers the same fundamental note as the 6-hole barrel. However, some drone barrels are tuned to other notes in the standard barrel's scale, offering a different experience from the fundamental note tuning.

When crafting a drone flute, remember that the two sound chambers *must* be the same length and the sound holes for the two barrels *must* be identical in measurement and placement to ensure the fundamental note and second octave of each barrel play in tune with the fundamental and octave of the other barrel.

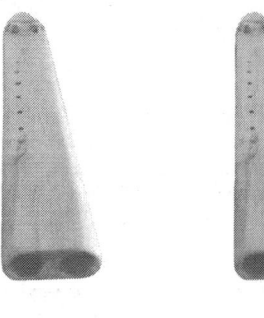

Craft the Drone Flute

The drone will require two birds, one for each channel. See Chapter Seven for instructions.

Materials

- two 1/2 x 4 x 24-inch hobby boards, available in pine, poplar, oak, and other woods, depending on store stock, or 1/2 x 4 x 24-inch aromatic cedar planks (If you prefer another size, such as 3/4-inch thick, the directions that follow can be easily adapted. I utilize wood from naturally-downed trees and hobby board.)
- two pieces 2 x 2 x 1-inch pine or cedar wood (birds)
- leather, twine, or other string to secure birds to flute
- two corks or wood dowels the size of channel bore, approximately 1/2-inch long
- carpenter's glue
- fine, medium, coarse sandpaper
- finishing oil (linseed, tung oil, etc.)
- spray lacquer, varnish, paint, or other finish (optional)

Tools

- electronic chromatic tuner (tuning applications for computers and smartphones provide an excellent alternative to a stand-alone tuner)
- electric sander (optional)

- ❧ tape measure
- ❧ small handsaw or hacksaw
- ❧ table saw
- ❧ 24-inch straightedge
- ❧ 4 to 8 wood clamps
- ❧ 3-inch trimming hand plane
- ❧ electric router
- ❧ router table
- ❧ 3/4-inch core box router bit
- ❧ rotary tool and/or high-speed drill
- ❧ 1/8-inch drill bit
- ❧ 1/4-inch flat and rounded needle files
- ❧ homemade sanding rod (see Chapter Six or Chapter Eight for instructions)

Router Setup

1. Attach the router to the router table according to manufacturer instructions.

2. Mark one end of the wood to be routed for a bit height of 3/8-inch.

3. Place the wood on the router table with the marked end against the router bit.

4. Adjust the router bit up or down so that the midpoint on top rests at the mark on the wood.

5. Set the router table guide to ensure at least a 1/4-inch wall between the router guide and flute channel. (Adjust the at least 1-3/8-inch to ensure a 1/4-inch wall between the two barrels when routing the second barrel.)

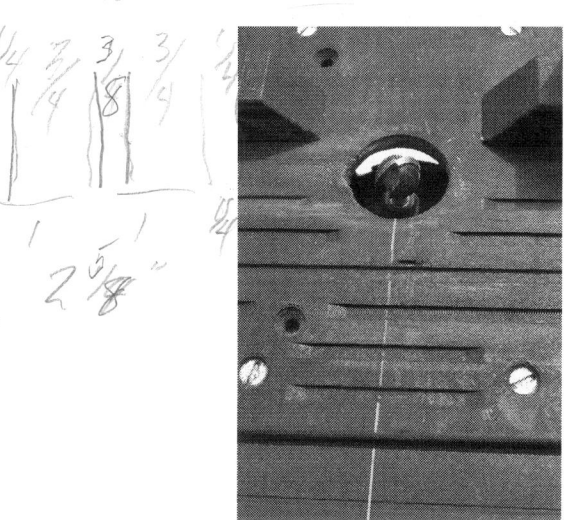

6. With a straightedge draw a line from the midpoint of the router bit to the table side to act as a channel routing stop-point guide.

Craft the Flute

Photographs of the crafting process follow these instructions.

1. Mark the wood two inches from one end to serve as

stopping point for channel routing.

2. Rout a channel into the first plank from the foot end to the marked point, switch off power to the router, and remove wood.

3. Rout a channel into the second plank from the foot end to the marked point, switch off power to the router, and remove wood.

4. Shift the table routing guide at least 1-3/8-inch away from the routing bit to ensure 1/4-inch or more space between the channels.

5. Rout the second channel in the first and second planks from the foot end to the marked point, switch off power to the router, and remove wood.

6. If hobby board is used, rip the sides of the planks lengthwise with a table saw or handsaw, ensuring at least 1/4-inch thick channel side walls.

7. With sandpaper wrapped around a dowel for more uniform sanding, fine-sand the channel halves to ensure a smooth surface. Do not sand channel rim contact points.

8. Approximately 1-1/5 to 2 inches from mouthpiece end of each channel, insert the plugs. Placement of plugs *must* match exactly to ensure

proper tuning. Use either a correctly sized dowel or cork for the plug. I prefer cork for its flexibility.

9. Mark placement of sound holes and air holes. Placement in first barrel must match placement in second barrel exactly.

10. Drill 1/8-inch sound and air holes.

11. Apply glue to the halves and, careful not to shift the plugs, assemble the halves to form the flute body.

12. Clamp the flute and allow 24 hours to dry.

13. Mark guide for drilling mouthpiece holes, angling to ensure close proximity for ease of playing.

14. Square the sound and air holes to 1/4-inch, making certain each hole matches its counterpart's size and placement exactly.

17. Shape the foot underside of both sound holes to 45-degree, 1/16-inch thick blunt edges.

18. Craft and secure the birds. Refer to Chapter Seven for bird crafting instructions.

19. Test the flute for sound, fine-adjusting the fetishes, splitting edges, and air holes until the desired sound is achieved.

If the sound is too airy, reduce the channel depth. If airflow is restricted, increase the depth. Make sure the fetishes are seated properly over the air holes and at the mouthpiece side of the sound holes. If no note is produced, check the labium for uniformity and anomalies. You may have to experiment.

20. With the tuner, determine the pitch/note of the current length and shorten the barrels incrementally (no more than 1/4-inch each time) to attain the desired fundamental note/flute key.

21. Choose the barrel you prefer as the melody flute.

22. With a straightedge, draw a guideline for finger hole placement from the middle of the labium to the flute's foot.

23. Determine and mark finger-hole placement by using the following hole placement percentages and formula:

Sound Chamber Length (from sound hole to foot) x Percentage = Hole Placement

- hole 1, 64.5 percent from sound hole
- hole 2, 58 percent
- hole 3, 51 percent
- hole 4, 44 percent*
- hole 5, 38 percent
- hole 6, 31 percent

*For a 5-hole flute, do not drill the number 4 hole. Refer to tuning charts to see how the fourth hole omission affects the tuning of holes five and six. Placement percentages for other holes remain the same as those of the 6-hole flute.

24. Drill first hole no larger than 1/8-inch. Determine pitch. It should be lower than desired.

25. With a half-round or round needle file, raise the pitch by enlarging the hole slightly, primarily toward the sides and sound hole, testing frequently until the desired pitch has been reached.

26. Continue with the remaining holes, bringing each to desired pitch before proceeding to the next.

27. Fine-sand each hole to remove fragments. Do not enlarge holes further after attaining correct pitch.

28. With the small hand planer, rough-shape the wood, rounding the sides and angling the mouthpiece. As a guide, draw a circle the thickness desired—1/8-inch to 1/4-inch—around the foot and mouthpiece bores. With the hand planer, plane to those marks from about two inches from the foot end. For the mouthpiece, angle only from the 2-inch mark, careful not to plane into the air chamber which would render the flute useless.

29. With a hand sander, bench sander, rotary sander (such as a drill with sanding attachment), or by hand (which will take considerable time), fine shape the barrel sides, rounding as best as possible, beginning with coarse paper, followed by medium and fine grades.

30. Fine-sand both interior and exterior of the flute. Use the homemade sanding rod for interior.

31. Apply pre-finish if desired, including stain or oil such as tung or linseed. Allow oil or stain to dry 24 hours before proceeding to the final steps.

32. With a clean cloth, remove remaining dust from the interior and exterior.

33. Finish the flute as desired. I prefer spray lacquer, applying it first to the barrel interior. After drying (usually 45 minutes is sufficient), apply a coat to the exterior. Apply a second coat after the first has dried sufficiently. Allow the final coat to dry for at least 24 hours.

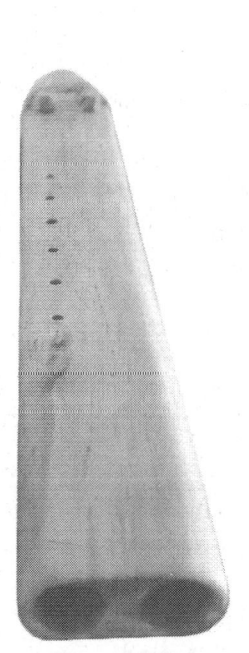
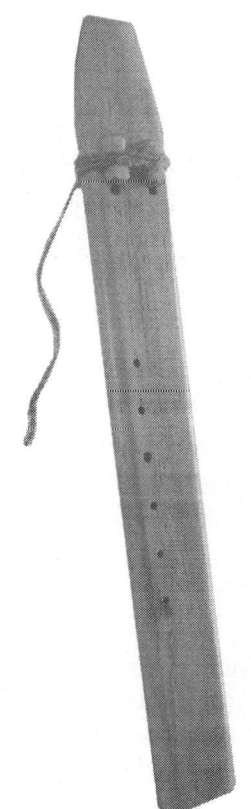
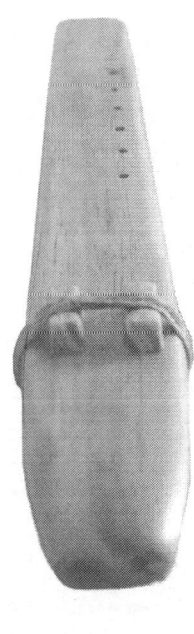

Craft the Drone Illustrated

Mark routing stop point.

Rout first channel.

Adjust guide for 1/4-inch wall between flute channels.

Complete channel routing.

Sand channels.

Measure for plug placement.

Drill air and sound holes.

Assemble halves.

Shape the air and sound holes.

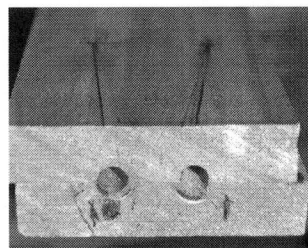

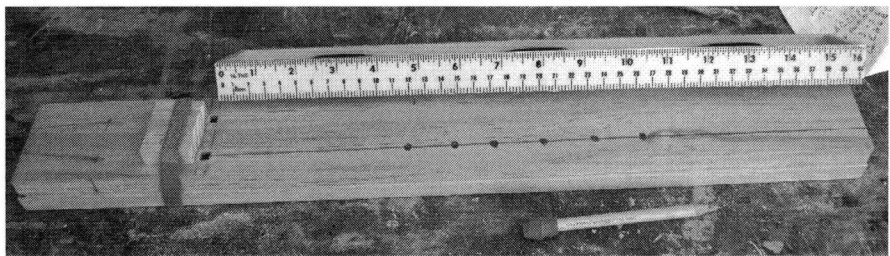

Drill mouthpiece holes.   *Calculate and mark finger hole placement.*

Drill finger holes, one by one, tuning each before moving to the next.

Shape with hand planer. Sand interior and exterior. Apply finish as desired.

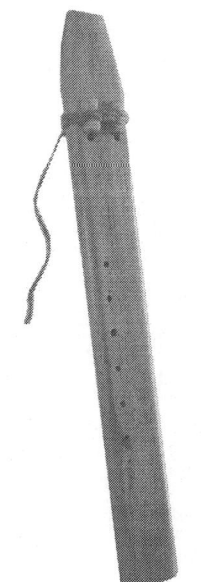

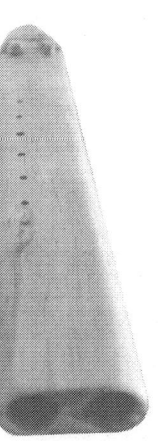

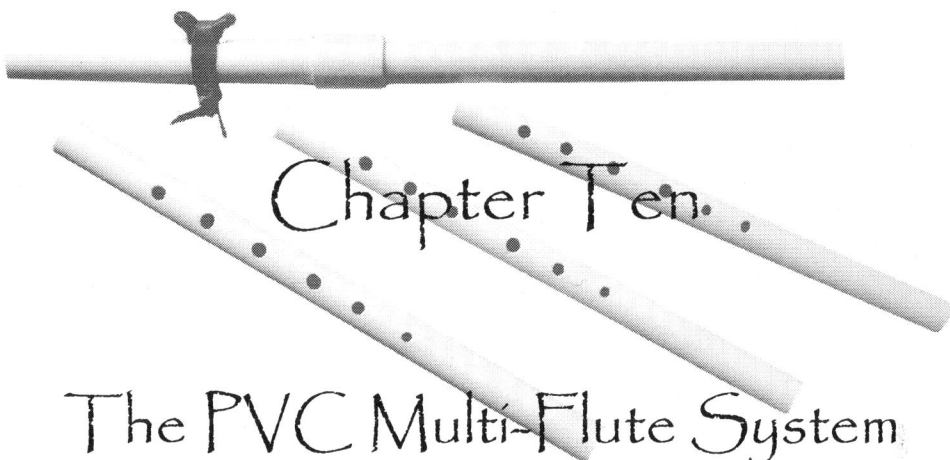

Chapter Ten

The PVC Multi-Flute System

The most difficult challenges for me in crafting a Native American flute are the bird, nest, and air hole. It takes *forever* to get these three components to produce a sound with which I'm pleased before moving on to tune the flute to its fundamental note and drill the finger holes. I play conventional transverse flute, which requires disassembly and cleaning after each session. As I put the flute away one day, I wondered whether a similar configuration could be implemented with the Native American flute to accommodate multiple barrels of varying lengths, utilizing one headjoint to create several flutes in different keys.

The following instructions are the result of my attempt to craft multiple flutes without the necessity of crafting multiple birds, nests, and air holes. The system incorporates the four flute keys I prefer—E, F, F#, and G—crafted with 3/4-inch PVC pipe. Barrels for G# and A could also be crafted with 3/4-inch pipe, creating a six-barrel system. An

A's sixth finger hole, however, may be too close to the connector to play the note adequately.

To craft the fetish/bird, please refer to the instructions in Chapter Seven.

Always wear an adequate dust mask or respirator when working with PVC.

Photographs of the crafting process follow these instructions.

Materials:

- 8-foot length 3/4-inch diameter PVC pipe
- one 3/4-inch PVC pipe connector (two if crafting slide-on fetish)
- 2 x 2 x 1-inch wood for wood fetish
- leather or other ties if wooden fetish utilized
- 3/4-inch diameter cork
- 6-inch length 1/2-inch to 5/8-inch diameter dowel or other

tool to slide cork into fetish
- fine-grade sandpaper
- fine-grade steel wool
- cleanser

Tools:

9'4

- 24-inch straightedge
- electronic chromatic tuner
- fine-tooth handsaw
- rotary tool
- 1/8-inch rotary tool drill bit
- flat fine-tooth wood file
- 1/4-inch wide needle files
- sanding rod
- sanding block

Craft the Headjoint

1. Cut a 9-5/32-inch length of PVC pipe.

2. Slide one end of the cut PVC pipe into the connector to rest tightly against the connector's divider lip.

3. From the mouthpiece end, opposite the connector end, measure 4-5/8 inches and mark the PVC for the air hole.

4. From the mouthpiece end, measure 5-3/16 inches and mark the PVC for the sound hole in line with the air hole.

5. With the rotary tool, drill 1/8-inch the air and sound holes.

6. Cut cork to fit between the holes.

7. Slide the cork into position be-

tween holes.

8. Square the holes to 1/4-inch. The air hole can be rounded if preferred.

9. Shape the sound hole's foot underside to a 45-degree, 1/16-inch thick blunt edge.

34. Use the sanding block or wood file to flatten the barrel between the sound and air holes from 1/4-inch beyond each hole. Flatten enough to form the rectangular nest, about 3/16-inch wide.

10. If a slide-on fetish is utilized, check the sound often to ensure the nest does not become too flat.

11. Use fine-grade sandpaper to smooth the nest, air hole, and sound hole.

12. With the sanding rod, remove remnants from the interior chamber.

13. Clean the factory writing from the PVC with water, cleanser, and fine-grade steel wool.

14. Dry the exterior and interior with a soft absorbent cloth.

15. When you have achieved the desired sound and cleaned the headjoint, proceed to crafting the barrels.

Craft the Barrels

Flutes based on the measurements

below may play sharp or flat, depending on the fetish, the sound hole, and the exact position of the barrel in the connector. Make certain a barrel is fully seated against the connector's interior lip. If a flute is properly seated and plays sharp, cut a longer barrel but save the sharp barrel for a higher key. Seat the longer barrel and shorten it by increments until achieving the target fundamental. Then calculate and drill finger holes using the formula and percentages in Chapter Eight.

G Barrel

1. Cut a 11-15/32-inch length of PVC.

2. Use sandpaper to reduce the exterior diameter of the connecting end. Reduction will ensure a tight but manageable fit of the barrel in the connector.

3. Insert the barrel into the headjoint connector. Make sure it is fully seated against the connector's interior lip.

4. Determine the fundamental note and decide if adjustment is required.

5. If required, make necessary adjustments and calculations. If adjustment is not required, use the straightedge to mark the barrel from the sound hole to the foot as a guide for finger-hole placement.

6. Along the guide line, *measuring from the foot toward the sound hole*, mark the finger hole positions at the following points *only if no adjustments are required to the length of the barrel*. If adjustments are required to the barrel length, use the percentages and formula in Chapter Eight to calculate proper finger hole placement.

- hole 1: Bb, 4-7/32 inches
- hole 2: C, 5-3/8 inches
- hole 3: D, 6-11/16 inches
- hole 4: E, 8-1/16 inches
- hole 5: F#, 9-5/32 inches
- hole 6: G#, 10-5/32 inches

7. Drill hole 1. Using a rounded needle file, enlarge the hole to the desired pitch. Proceed to successive holes one by one.

8. After drilling and tuning, remove PVC remnants from the barrel's interior with the sanding rod.

9. Fine-sand all holes, careful not to enlarge them further, clean the barrel, and proceed to crafting the next barrel.

F# Barrel

1. Cut a 12-19/32-inch length of PVC.

2. Use sandpaper to reduce the exterior diameter of the connecting end.

3. Fully seat the barrel into the headjoint connector.

4. Determine the fundamental note and decide if adjustment is required.

5. If required, make necessary adjustments and calculations. If adjustment is not required, use the straightedge to mark the barrel from the sound hole to the foot as a guide for finger-hole placement.

6. Along the guide line, *measuring from the foot toward the sound hole*, mark the finger hole positions at the following points *only if no adjustments are required to the length of the barrel*. If adjustments are required to the barrel length, use the percentages and formula in Chapter Eight to calculate proper finger hole placement.

   ➤ hole 1: A, 5-3/32 inches A
   ➤ hole 2: B, 5-15/16 inches
   ➤ hole 3: C#, 7-1/4 inches
   ➤ hole 4: Eb, 8-19/32 inches
   ➤ hole 5: F, 10-5/32 inches
   ➤ hole 6: G, 10-27/32 inches

7. Drill hole 1. Using a rounded needle file, enlarge the hole to the desired pitch. Proceed to successive holes one by one.

8. After drilling and tuning, remove PVC remnants from the barrel's interior with the sanding rod.

9. Fine-sand all holes, careful not to enlarge them further, clean the barrel, and proceed to crafting the next barrel.

F Barrel

1. Cut a 13-13/32-inch length of PVC.

2. Use sandpaper to reduce the exterior diameter of the connecting end.

3. Fully seat the barrel into the headjoint.

4. Determine the fundamental note and decide if adjustment is required.

5. If required, make necessary adjustments and calculations. If adjustment is not required, use the straightedge to mark the barrel from the sound hole to the foot as a guide for finger-hole placement.

6. Along the guide line, *measuring from the foot toward the sound hole*, mark the finger hole positions at the following points *only if no adjustments are required to the length of the barrel*. If adjustments are required to the barrel length, use the percentages and formula in Chapter Eight to calculate proper finger hole placement.

   ➤ hole 1: G#, 5-1/32 inches
   ➤ hole 2: Bb, 6-1/4 inches
   ➤ hole 3: C, 7-9/16 inches
   ➤ hole 4: D, 9-1/8 inches
   ➤ hole 5: E, 10-9/32 inches
   ➤ hole 6: F#, 11-1/2 inches

7. Drill hole 1. Using a rounded

needle file, enlarge the hole to the desired pitch. Proceed to successive holes one by one.

8. After drilling and tuning, remove PVC remnants from the barrel's interior with the sanding rod.

9. Fine-sand all holes, careful not to enlarge them further, clean the barrel, and proceed to crafting the next barrel.

E Barrel

1. Cut a 14-23/32-inch length of PVC.

2. Use sandpaper to reduce the exterior diameter of the connecting end.

3. Fully seat the barrel into the headjoint connector.

4. Determine the fundamental note and decide if adjustment is required.

5. If required, make necessary adjustments and calculations. If adjustment is not required, use the straightedge to mark the barrel from the sound hole to the foot as a guide for finger-hole placement.

6. Along the guide line, *measur-ing from the foot toward the sound hole*, mark the finger hole positions at the following points *only if no adjustments are required to the length of the barrel*. If adjustments are required to the barrel length, use the percentages and formula in Chapter Eight to calculate proper finger

- hole 1: G, 5-1/32 inches G
- hole 2: A, 6-15/32 inches
- hole 3: B, 7-11/16 inches
- hole 4: C#, 9-5/32 inches
- hole 5: D#, 10-19/32 inches
- hole 6: F, 11-15/16 inches

7. Drill hole 1. Using a rounded needle file, enlarge the hole to the desired pitch. Proceed to successive holes one by one.

8. After drilling and tuning, remove PVC remnants from the barrel's interior with the sanding rod.

9. Fine-sand all holes, careful not to enlarge them further.

If you haven't already done so, clean all barrels with water, cleanser, and fine-grade steel wool to remove factory lettering. Dry the interior and exterior with a soft, absorbent cloth. If desired, apply a finish such as lacquer or paint.

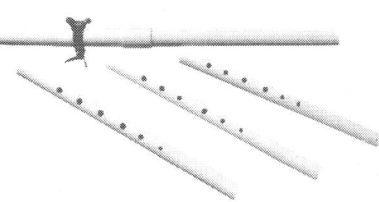

Craft the PVC Multi-Barrel System Illustrated

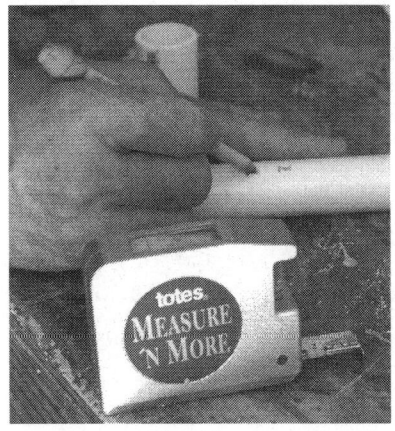

Measure for air and sound holes.

Drill air and sound holes.

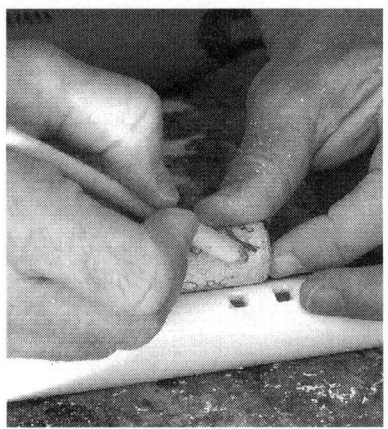

Measure for plug.

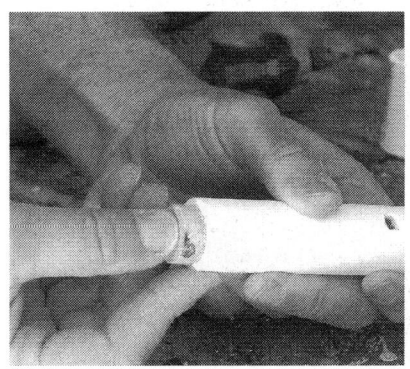

Insert plug

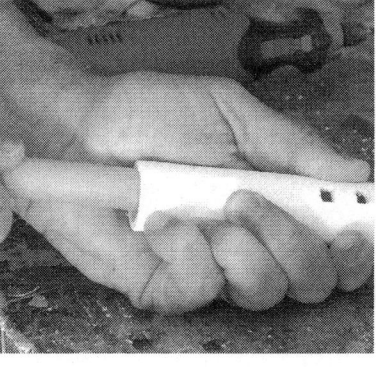

Move plug into position between air and sound holes.

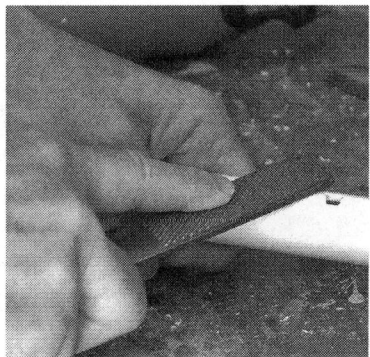

Flatten nest.

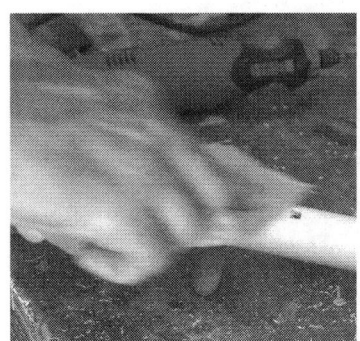

Smooth nest.

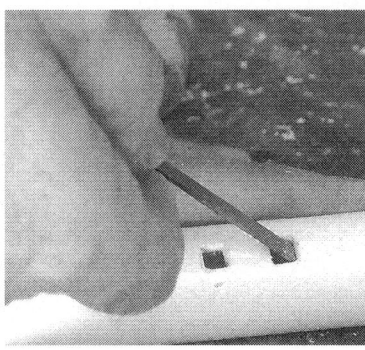

Shape air and sound holes.

Clean the finished headjoint.

Reduce barrel exterior diameter for proper seating in headjoint.

Cut barrel to size. Make adjustments if sharp or flat.

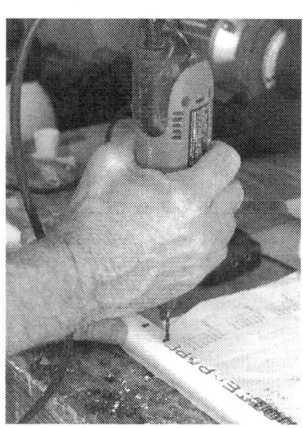

Drill first finger hole.

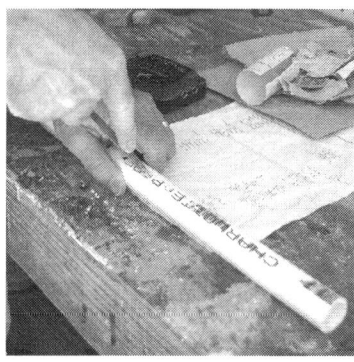

Tune each finger hole before moving to next.

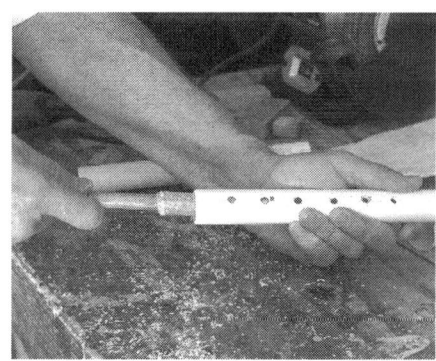

Clean interior remnants with sanding rod.

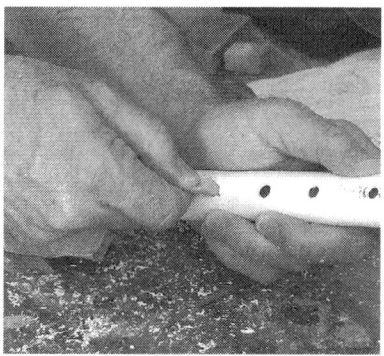

Fine sand finger holes and clean all barrels.

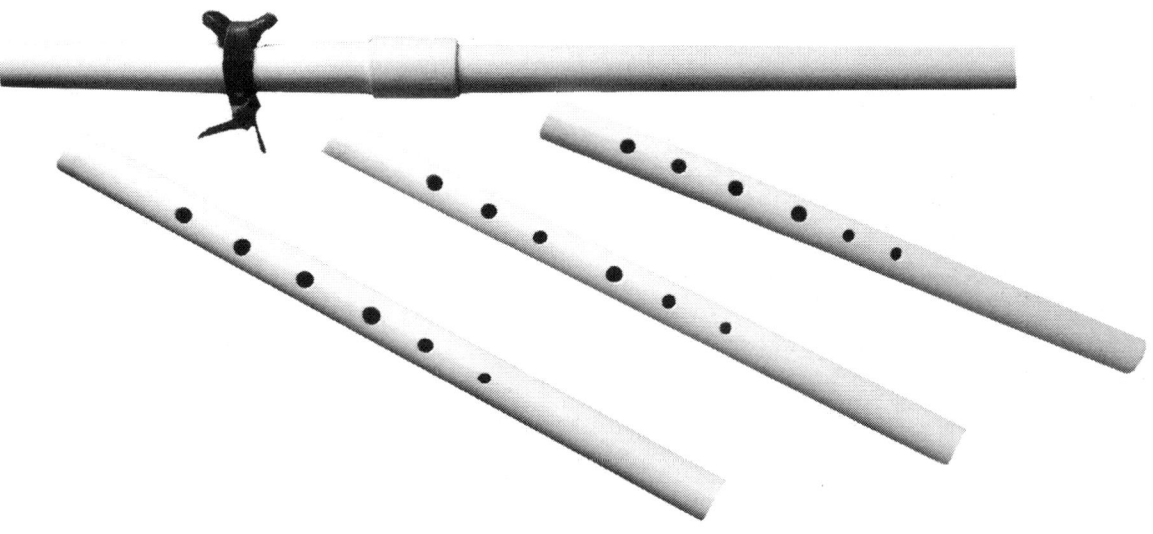

Chapter Eleven

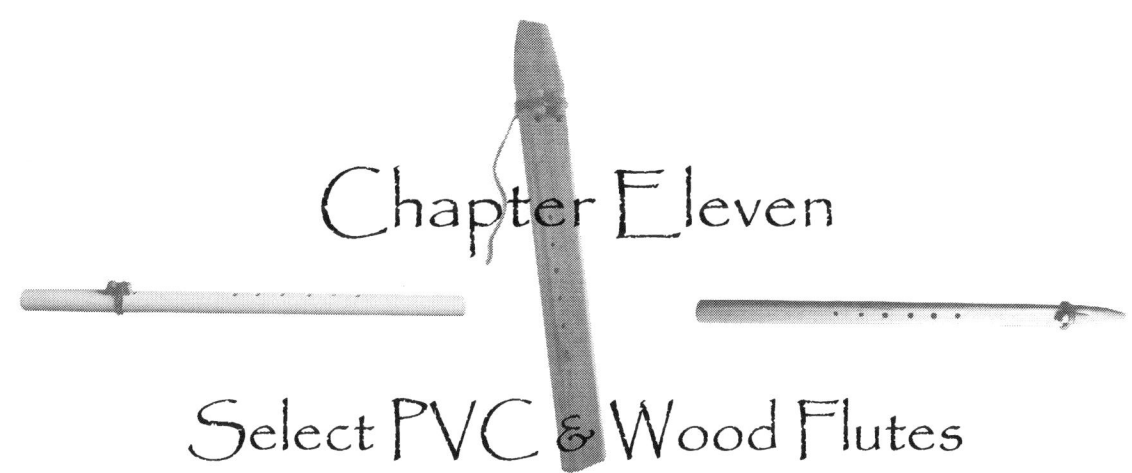

Select PVC & Wood Flutes

Preceding chapters provide the formula and percentages that can be used to craft flutes of varying lengths, diameters, and keys. This chapter is dedicated to flutes of predefined dimensions, eliminating the need for calculation to determine finger hole placement. In general, even for flutes that require mathematical calculation to determine hole placement, the following basic measurements are utilized for all modern Native American flutes I craft. These measurements, however, can be amended to fit specific needs and preferences:

- air hole: 1/4-inch square or circle
- sound hole: 1/4-inch square
- labium: 45-degree underside, 1/16-inch blunt edge
- channel: 1/16-inch deep, 1/4-inch wide
- flute wall thickness: 5/16-inch

PVC Flute

Please refer to Chapter Seven for instructions to craft the bird. For your convenience, Chapter Eight's illustrated PVC flute crafting instructions are included in this chapter.

Materials

- 2 x 2 x 1-inch wood for fetish, or 3/4-inch PVC pipe connector for slide-on fetish
- leather, twine, or other string to secure wood bird to flute
- 24-inch length of PVC in the following diameters:
  - A, B, and C flutes: 1/2-inch diameter
  - Low C# flute: 1-1/4-inch diameter
  - E, F, F#, and Anasazi flute: 3/4-inch diameter
- appropriate diameter cork or

plastic knockout plug (refer to Chapter Twelve for more information about knockout plugs)
- dowel or other tool to slide cork or knockout plug into pipe
- fine-grade sandpaper
- steel wool
- cleanser
- lacquer or paint (optional)

Tools

- 24-inch straightedge
- electronic chromatic tuner (tuning applications for computers and smartphones provide an excellent alternative to a stand-alone tuner)
- rotary tool
- 1/8-inch rotary tool drill bit
- flat fine-tooth wood file
- 1/4-inch round and flat needle files
- sanding rod
- sanding block

Craft the A Flute

1. Cut an 18-1/8-inch length of 1/2-inch diameter PVC pipe.

2. Mark the slow air chamber hole placement at 3-13/16 inches from mouthpiece end.

3. Mark the sound hole placement at 4-1/2 inches from mouthpiece end.

4. With the rotary tool and 1/8-inch bit, drill the air and sound holes.

5. Cut the cork to fit between the sound and air holes, or trim off the knockout plug flange.

6. Using the dowel, slide the cork or plug into position between the sound and air holes.

7. Square the air and sound holes to no more than 1/4-inch. The air hole can be rounded if preferred.

8. Shape the sound hole's foot underside to a 45-degree angle to form a 1/16-inch thick blunt edge.

9. Use the sanding block or wood file to flatten the barrel between the sound and air holes from 1/4-inch beyond each hole. Flatten enough to form the rectangular nest, about 3/16-inch wide.

10. Affix the fetish.

11. Determine the fundamental note and whether any adjustments to the fetish or sound chamber length are required.

12. If the fundamental note is flat, shorten the sound chamber in small increments to raise the fundamental. If the fundamental is sharp, either start with a new, longer piece of PVC or adjust the pitch of each finger hole to the same degree of sharpness as the fundamental.

13. If adjustment is not required, use the straightedge to mark the barrel from the sound hole to the foot as a guide for finger hole placement.

14. Along the guide line and *measuring from the foot toward the sound hole*, mark the finger hole positions at the following points *only if no adjustments to the length of the barrel have been required*. If adjustments have been made, then use the percentages and formula in Chapter Eight to calculate hole placement.

    - hole 1: C, 3-11/16 inches
    - hole 2: D, 4-5/8 inches
    - hole 3: E, 5-1/2 inches
    - hole 4: F#, 6-23/32 inches
    - hole 5: G#, 7-9/16 inches
    - hole 6: Bb, 8-3/4 inches

15. Drill hole 1.

16. Using a rounded needle file, enlarge the hole until achieving the desired pitch, and then proceed to the next hole.

17. Clean remnants from the interior chambers with the sanding rod. Clean remnants from each finger hole with fine-grade sandpaper, careful not to enlarge the holes any further.

18. Clean the flute with water, cleanser, and fine-grade steel wool to remove factory lettering. Dry the interior and exterior with a soft, absorbent cloth.

19. Finish with lacquer or paint if desired.

Craft the B Flute

1. Cut a 15-inch length of 1/2-inch diameter PVC pipe.

2. Mark air hole placement at 2-3/8 inches from mouthpiece end.

3. Mark for sound hole placement at 2-15/16 inches a from mouthpiece end.

4. With the rotary tool and 1/8-inch bit, drill the air and sound holes.

5. Cut the cork to fit between the sound and air holes, or trim off the knockout plug flange.

6. Using the dowel, slide the cork or plug into position between the sound and air holes.

7. Square the air and sound holes to no more than 1/4-inch. The air hole can be rounded if preferred.

8. Shape the sound hole's foot underside to a 45-degree angle to form a 1/16-inch thick blunt edge.

9. Use the sanding block or wood file to flatten the barrel between the sound and air holes from 1/4-inch beyond each hole. Flatten enough to form the rectangular nest,

about 3/16-inch wide.

10. Affix the fetish.

11. Determine the fundamental note and if any adjustments to the fetish or sound chamber length are required.

12. If the fundamental note is flat, shorten the sound chamber in small increments to raise the fundamental. If the fundamental is sharp, either start with a new, longer piece of PVC or adjust the pitch of each finger hole to the same degree of sharpness as the fundamental.

13. If adjustment is not required, use the straightedge to mark the barrel from the sound hole to the foot as a guide for finger hole placement.

14. Along the guide line and *measuring from the foot toward the sound hole*, mark the finger hole positions at the following points *only if no adjustments to the length of the barrel have been required*. If adjustments have been made, then use the percentages and formula in Chapter Eight to calculate hole placement.

  - hole 1: D, 3-13/16 inches
  - hole 2: E, 4-11/16 inches
  - hole 3: F#, 5-1/2 inches
  - hole 4: G#, 6-7/16 inches
  - hole 5: Bb, 7-5/16 inches
  - hole 6: C, 8-3/16 inches

15. Drill hole 1.

16. Using a rounded needle file, enlarge the hole until achieving the desired pitch, and then proceed to the next hole.

17. Clean remnants from each hole with fine-grade sandpaper, careful not to enlarge the holes any further.

18. Clean all barrels with water, cleanser, and fine-grade steel wool to remove factory lettering. Dry the interior and exterior with a soft, absorbent cloth.

19. Finish with lacquer or paint if desired.

Craft the C Flute

1. Cut a 14-1/4-inch length of 1/2-inch diameter PVC pipe.

2. Mark for the air hole at 2-1/2 inches from mouthpiece end.

3. Mark for the sound hole at 2-15/16 inches from mouthpiece end.

4. With the rotary tool and 1/8-inch bit, drill the air and sound holes.

5. Cut the cork to fit between the sound and air holes, or trim off the knockout plug flange.

6. Using the long dowel, slide the cork or plug into position between the sound and air holes.

7. Square the air and sound holes to no more than 1/4-inch. The air hole can be rounded if preferred.

8. File the underside of sound hole's foot side to a roughly 45-degree angle, creating a blunt splitting edge 1/16 inch thick.

9. Use the sanding block or wood file to flatten the barrel between the sound and air holes from 1/4-inch beyond each hole. Flatten enough to form the rectangular nest, about 3/16-inch wide.

10. Affix the fetish.

11. Determine the fundamental note and whether any adjustments to the fetish or sound chamber length. are required.

12. If the fundamental note is flat, shorten the sound chamber in small increments to raise the fundamental. If the fundamental is sharp, either start with a new, longer piece of PVC or adjust the pitch of each finger hole to the same degree of sharpness as the fundamental.

13. If adjustment is not required, use the straightedge to mark the barrel from the sound hole to the foot as a guide for finger hole placement.

14. Along the guide line and *measuring from the foot toward the sound hole*, mark the finger hole positions at the following points *only if no adjustments to the length of the barrel have been required*. If adjustments have been made, then use the percentages and formula in Chapter Eight to calculate hole placement.

- hole 1: Eb, 3-7/16 inches
- hole 2: F, 4-1/4 inches
- hole 3: G, 4-15/16 inches
- hole 4: A, 5-7/8 inches
- hole 5: B, 6-3/4 inches
- hole 6: C#, 7-9/16 inches

15. Drill hole 1.

16. Using a rounded needle file, enlarge the hole until achieving the desired pitch, and then proceed to the next hole.

17. Clean remnants from each hole with fine-grade sandpaper, careful not to enlarge the holes any further.

18. Clean all barrels with water, cleanser, and fine-grade steel wool to remove factory lettering. Dry the interior and exterior with a soft, absorbent cloth.

19. Finish with lacquer or paint if desired.

Craft the E flute

1. Cut a 21-1/2-inch length of 3/4-inch diameter PVC pipe.

2. Mark for air hole placement at

3-3/4 inches from mouthpiece end.

3. Mark for sound hole placement at 4-1/2 inches from mouthpiece end.

4. With the rotary tool and 1/8-inch bit, drill the air and sound holes.

5. Cut the cork to fit between the sound and air holes, or trim off the knockout plug flange.

6. Using the long dowel, slide the cork or plug into position between the sound and air holes.

7. Square the air and sound holes to no more than 1/4-inch. The air hole can be rounded if preferred.

8. File the underside of sound hole's foot side to a roughly 45-degree angle to form a blunt splitting edge 1/16 inch thick.

9. Use the sanding block or wood file to flatten the barrel between the sound and air holes from 1/4-inch beyond each hole. Flatten enough to form the rectangular nest, about 3/16-inch wide.

10. Affix the fetish.

11. Determine the fundamental note and whether any adjustments to the fetish or sound chamber length. are required.

12. If the fundamental note is flat, shorten the sound chamber in small increments to raise the fundamental. If the fundamental is sharp, either start with a new, longer piece of PVC or adjust the pitch of each finger hole to the same degree of sharpness as the fundamental.

13. If adjustment is not required, use the straightedge to mark the barrel from the sound hole to the foot as a guide for finger hole placement.

14. Along the guide line and *measuring from the foot toward the sound hole*, mark the finger hole positions at the following points *only if no adjustments to the length of the barrel have been required*. If adjustments have been made, then use the percentages and formula in Chapter Eight to calculate hole placement.

    - hole 1: G, 6-1/4 inches
    - hole 2: A, 7-3/8 inches
    - hole 3: B, 8-9/16 inches
    - hole 4: C#, 9-15/16 inches
    - hole 5: Eb, 11-1/16 inches
    - hole 6: F, 12-1/4 inches

15. Drill hole 1.

16. Using a rounded needle file, enlarge the hole until achieving the desired pitch, and then proceed to the next hole.

17. Clean remnants from each hole with fine-grade sandpa-

per, careful not to enlarge the holes any further.

18. Clean all barrels with water, cleanser, and fine-grade steel wool to remove factory lettering. Dry the interior and exterior with a soft, absorbent cloth.

19. Finish with lacquer or paint if desired.

Craft the F Flute

1. Cut a 19-5/8-inch length of 3/4-inch diameter PVC pipe.

2. Mark for air hole placement at 2-5/8 inches from mouthpiece end.

3. Mark for sound hole placement at 3-1/2 inches from mouthpiece end.

4. With the rotary tool and 1/8-inch bit, drill the air and sound holes.

5. Cut the cork to fit between the sound and air holes, or trim off the knockout plug flange.

6. Using the long dowel, slide the cork or plug into position between the sound and air holes.

7. Square the two holes to no more than 1/4-inch. The air hole can be rounded if preferred.

8. File the underside of sound hole's foot side to a 45-degree angle to form a blunt splitting edge 1/16 inch thick.

9. Use the sanding block or wood file to flatten the barrel between the sound and air holes from 1/4-inch beyond each hole. Flatten enough to form the rectangular nest, about 3/16-inch wide.

10. Affix the fetish.

11. Determine the fundamental note and whether any adjustments to the fetish or sound chamber length. are required.

12. If the fundamental note is flat, shorten the sound chamber in small increments to raise the fundamental. If the fundamental is sharp, either start with a new, longer piece of PVC or adjust the pitch of each finger hole to the same degree of sharpness as the fundamental.

13. If adjustment is not required, use the straightedge to mark the barrel from the sound hole to the foot as a guide for finger hole placement.

14. Along the guide line and *measuring from the foot toward the sound hole*, mark the finger hole positions at the following points *only if no adjustments to the length of the barrel have been required*. If adjustments have been made, then use the percentages and formula in

Chapter Eight to calculate hole placement.

- ❧ hole 1: G#, 5-3/8 inches
- ❧ hole 2: Bb, 6-1/2 inches
- ❧ hole 3: C, 7-5/8 inches
- ❧ hole 4: D, 8-7/8 inches
- ❧ hole 5: E, 9-7/8 inches
- ❧ hole 6: F#, 11 inches

15. Drill hole 1.

16. Using a rounded needle file, enlarge the hole until achieving the desired pitch, and then proceed to the next hole.

17. Clean remnants from each hole with fine-grade sandpaper, careful not to enlarge the holes any further.

18. Clean all barrels with water, cleanser, and fine-grade steel wool to remove factory lettering. Dry the interior and exterior with a soft, absorbent cloth.

19. Finish with lacquer or paint if desired.

Craft the F# Flute

1. Cut a 21-1/4-inch length of 3/4-inch diameter PVC pipe.

2. Mark for air hole placement at 4-25/32 inches from mouthpiece end.

3. Mark for sound hole placement at 5-9/16 inches from mouthpiece end.

4. With the rotary tool and 1/8-inch bit, drill the air and sound holes.

5. Cut the cork to fit between the sound and air holes, or trim off the knockout plug flange.

6. Using the long dowel, slide the cork or plug into position between the sound and air holes.

7. Square the air and sound holes to no more than 1/4-inch. The air hole can be rounded if preferred.

8. File the underside of sound hole's foot side to a 45-degree angle to form a blunt splitting edge 1/16 inch thick.

9. Use the sanding block or wood file to flatten the barrel between the sound and air holes from 1/4-inch beyond each hole. Flatten enough to form the rectangular nest, about 3/16-inch wide.

10. Affix the fetish.

11. Determine the fundamental note and whether any adjustments to the fetish or sound chamber length. are required.

12. If the fundamental note is flat, shorten the sound chamber in small increments to raise the fundamental. If the fundamental is sharp, either start with a new, longer piece of PVC or adjust the pitch of

each finger hole to the same degree of sharpness as the fundamental.

13. If adjustment is not required, use the straightedge to mark the barrel from the sound hole to the foot as a guide for finger hole placement.

14. Along the guide line and *measuring from the foot toward the sound hole*, mark the finger hole positions at the following points *only if no adjustments to the length of the barrel have been required*. If adjustments have been made, then use the percentages and formula in Chapter Eight to calculate hole placement.

> ➤ hole 1: A, 5 inches
> ➤ hole 2: B, 6-1/8 inches
> ➤ hole 3: C#, 7-3/8 inches
> ➤ hole 4: Eb, 8-9/16 inches
> ➤ hole 5: F, 9-3/4 inches
> ➤ hole 6: G, 10-7/8 inches

15. Drill hole 1.

16. Using a rounded needle file, enlarge the hole until achieving the desired pitch, and then proceed to the next hole.

17. Clean remnants from each hole with fine-grade sandpaper, careful not to enlarge the holes any further.

18. Clean all barrels with water, cleanser, and fine-grade steel wool to remove factory lettering. Dry the interior and exterior with a soft, absorbent cloth.

19. Finish with lacquer or paint if desired.

Craft the Low C# Flute

1. Cut a 22-1/4-inch length of 1-1/4-inch diameter PVC pipe.

2. Mark for air hole placement at 4-1/8 inches from mouthpiece end.

3. Mark for sound hole placement at 5-1/16 inches from mouthpiece end.

4. With the rotary tool and 1/8-inch bit, drill the air and sound holes.

5. Cut the cork to fit between the sound and air holes, or trim off the knockout plug flange.

6. Using the long dowel, slide the cork or plug into position between the sound and air holes.

7. Square the air and sound holes to no more than 1/4-inch. The air hole can be rounded if preferred.

8. File the underside of the sound hole's foot side to a 45-degree angle to form a 1/16 inch blunt splitting edge.

9. Use the sanding block or wood file to flatten the barrel between the sound and air holes from 1/4-inch beyond

each hole. Flatten enough to form the rectangular nest, about 3/16-inch wide.

10 Affix the fetish.

11 Determine the fundamental note and whether any adjustments to the fetish or sound chamber length. are required.

12 If the fundamental note is flat, shorten the sound chamber in small increments to raise the fundamental. If the fundamental is sharp, either start with a new, longer piece of PVC or adjust the pitch of each finger hole to the same degree of sharpness as the fundamental.

13 If adjustment is not required, use the straightedge to mark the barrel from the sound hole to the foot as a guide for finger hole placement.

14 Along the guide line and *measuring from the foot toward the sound hole*, mark the finger hole positions at the following points *only if no adjustments to the length of the barrel have been required*. If adjustments have

[handwritten annotations: "if FLAT cut off" and "if # make longer"]

been made, then use the percentages and formula in Chapter Eight to calculate hole placement.

- hole 1: E, 6-1/4 inches
- hole 2: F#, 7-5/8 inches
- hole 3: G#, 9 inches
- hole 4: Bb, 10-1/2 inches
- hole 5: C, 11-7/8 inches
- hole 6: D, 13-11/32 inches

15. Drill hole 1.

16. Using a rounded needle file, enlarge the hole until achieving the desired pitch, and then proceed to the next hole.

17. Clean remnants from each hole with fine-grade sandpaper, careful not to enlarge the holes any further.

18. Clean all barrels with water, cleanser, and fine-grade steel wool to remove factory lettering. Dry the interior and exterior with a soft, absorbent cloth.

19. Finish with lacquer or paint if desired.

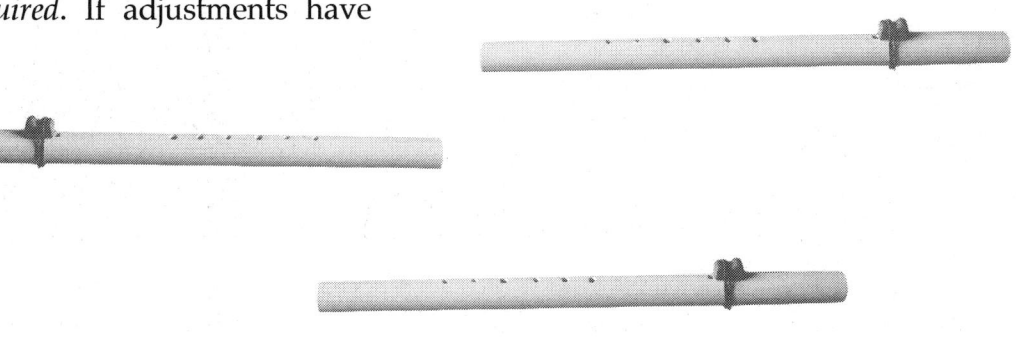

Craft the PVC Flute Illustrated

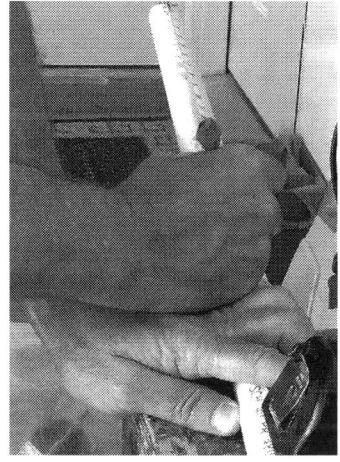

Measure a 24-inch length of PVC 3/4-inch diameter pipe.

With a fine-tooth saw, cut the length of pipe.

Drill the 1/8-inch air hole and sound hole according to specific flute directions.

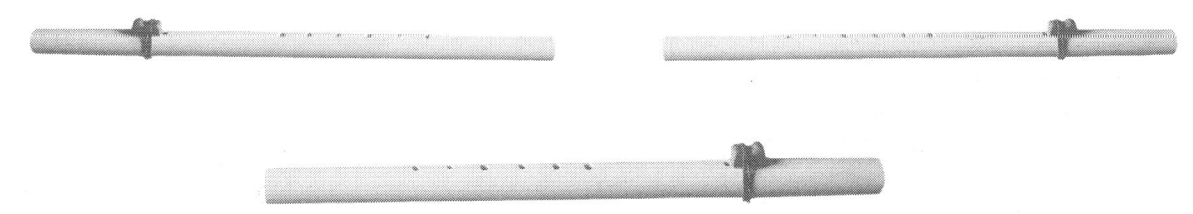

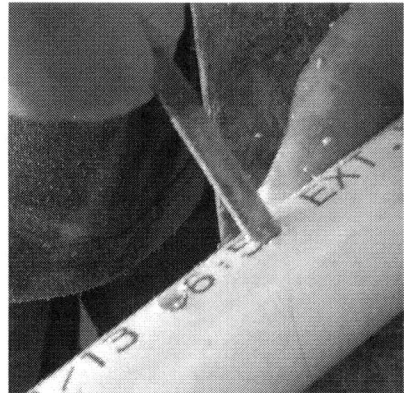
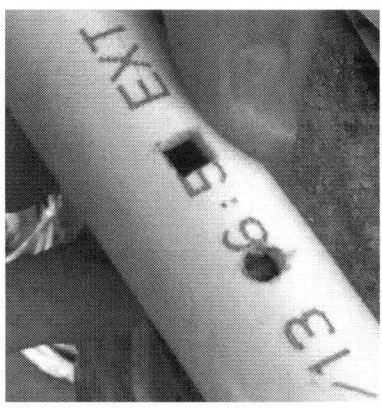
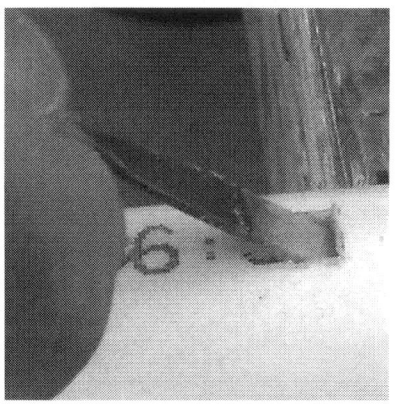

Shape inline the air and sound holes to 1/4-inch square.

The air hole can be round or square to desire.

Shape sound hole's foot underside at 45-degree angle to form 1/16-inch blunt edge.

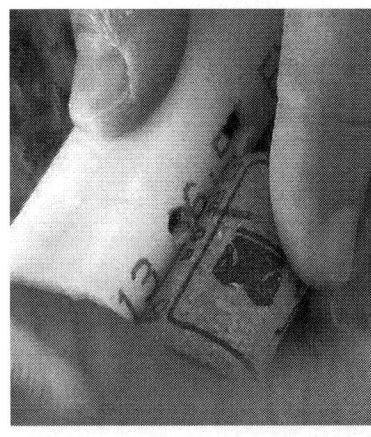

Measure cork or dowel for plug between air and sound holes.

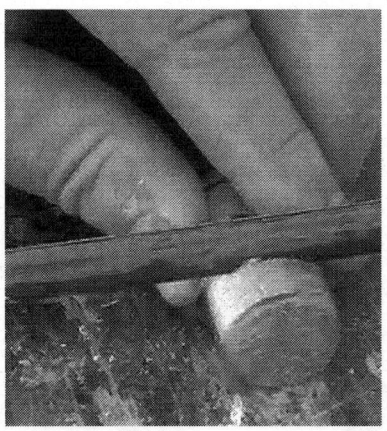

Cut cork or dowel.

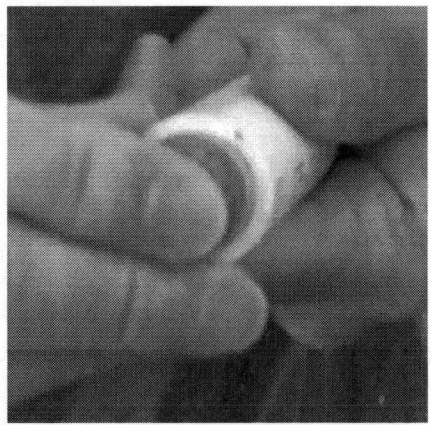

Insert cork or dowel into mouthpiece end.

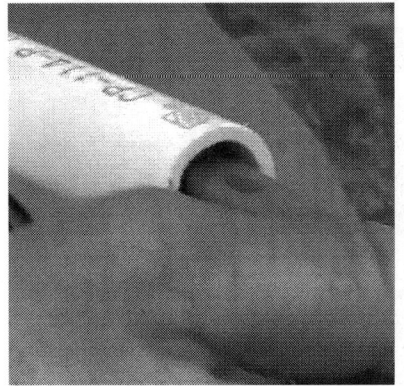

With blunt instrument, move the plug into place between air and sound holes.

Flatten the nest area.

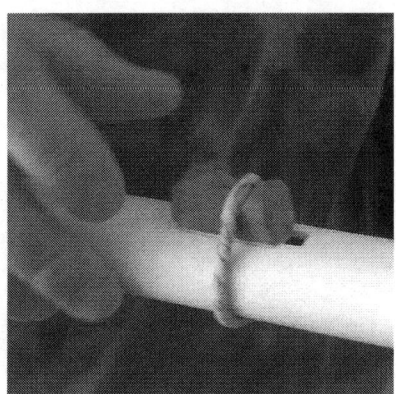

Secure the fetish and determine the fundamental note.

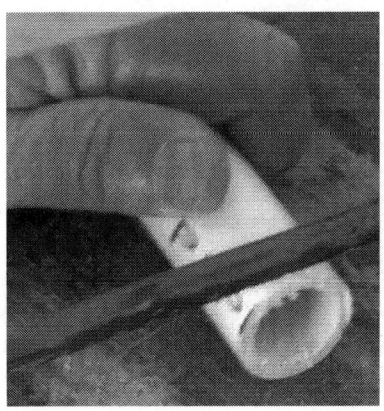

Shorten the pipe by increments to reach desired fundamental.

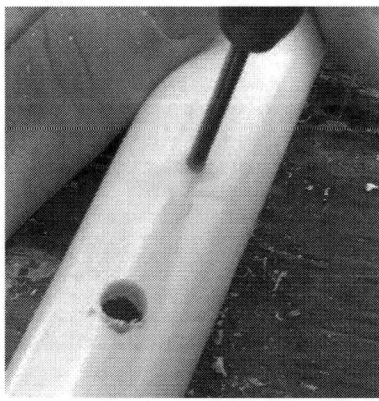

Calculate, mark, and drill the finger holes, tuning each before proceeding to the next.

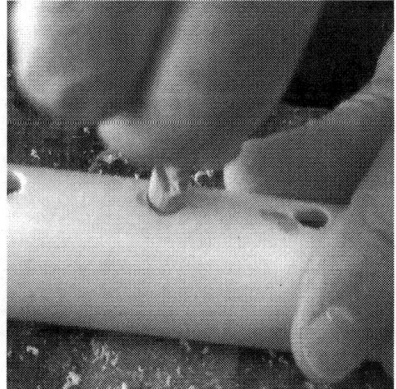

Remove remnants with fine sandpaper. Do not enlarge hole after reaching desired note.

Craft the PVC Anasazi Flute

For more information regarding the crafting of the Anasazi flute, please refer to Chapter Six.

1. Cut a 29-13/16-inch length of 3/4-inch diameter PVC pipe.

2. Cut the blowing end with a fine-tooth handsaw at a 25-degree angle.

3. Use a fine-tooth flat wood file to shape the blowing edge at a roughly 45-degree angle. As the edge sharpens, a "C" or oval shape will form. Try to keep the indentation to a depth of no more than 1/4-inch. The blowing edge should be sharp. Finish the edge with fine-grade sandpaper.

4. Clean the flute and blowing edge carefully of all dust. Practice blowing until you can produce a sustained low note on the flute.

5. With a straightedge, draw a line from middle of the blowing edge to the flute's foot end.

6. Measuring *from the foot*, mark placement of finger holes:

    *   From foot, hole 1: Bb, 4-7/8 inches
    *   hole 2: B, 6-1/2 inches
    *   hole 3: C, 8-1/8 inches
    *   hole 4: Eb, 12 inches
    *   hole 5: F, 13-9/16 inches
    *   hole 6: G, 15-5/16 inches

7. Use a high-speed rotary tool to drill holes. Drill hole 1 no larger than 1/8-inch. Do not proceed to the next hole. Determine hole 1's pitch, which should be lower than desired. With a half-round or round needle file, raise the pitch by enlarging the hole incrementally, primarily toward the sides and labium, testing frequently until the desired pitch has been attained. Proceed to the remaining holes, bringing each to desired pitch before proceeding to the next.

8. Fine-sand each hole to remove fragments. Do not enlarge holes any further after tuning to correct pitch.

9. To remove factory markings, scrub the PVC pipe with fine steel wool and a gentle scrubbing product. Rinse clean. Dry the interior and exterior. Finish the flute with spray lacquer or other spray paint as desired.

Wood Flutes

Modern Native American Flute

Minor variations in the interior diameter of wood flutes can result in flutes of the same key to be different lengths. Finger holes on one may also be placed at different points than finger holes on another. It's therefore best to calculate hole positions using the formula and percentages in Chapter Eight, based on sound chamber length.

If the wood is routed to an exact diameter matching those for the PVC flutes described above, then measurements used for the PVC flutes can be used for the corresponding wooden flutes. Be sure, however, to drill finger holes no larger than 1/8-inch and gradually enlarge them with a needle file until the desired pitch is reached.

The Drone Flute

If the two chambers are routed to an exact diameter of 3/4-inch, the following measurements can be used—again, starting with 1/8-inch finger holes and enlarging each gradually to correct pitch.

Follow the instructions for routing and assembling the drone flute body in Chapter Nine, but utilize the following measurements instead of the general percentages and formula. Remember, the length of each sound chamber must be *exactly* the same. The sound holes for the two barrels must also be *identical* in measurement and placement to ensure the fundamental notes of the barrels match in pitch.

- length: 20-3/8 inches
- from mouthpiece to start of sound chamber: 2 inches
- from mouthpiece to midpoint of air holes, 3-15/16 inches
- from mouthpiece to midpoint of sound holes, 4-11/16 inches
- interior barrel diameter: 3/4-inch
- fundamental note: F#
- *measuring from the foot end,* placement of finger holes:

  - Hole 1: A, 5-3/16 inches
  - Hole 2: B, 6-3/8 inches
  - Hole 3: C#, 7-9/16 inches
  - Hole 4: Eb, 8-13/16 inches
  - Hole 5: F, 10 inches
  - Hole 6: G, 11-1/8 inches

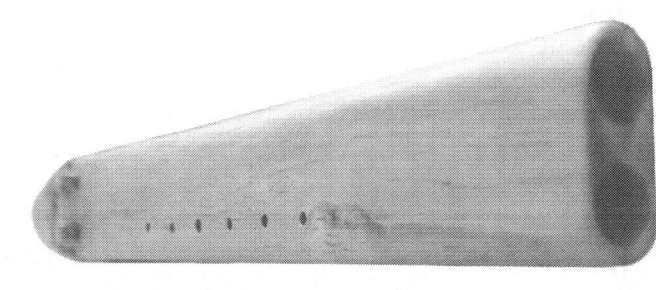

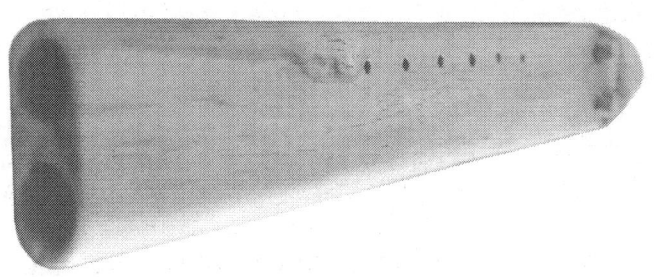

Chapter Twelve

Setback, Step Forward

Clay-tastrophe

The first source for research, reference, or entertainment most people turn to these days is the internet, which can prove an extraordinary repository of useful information or an infuriating collection of drivel. Case in point: I wanted to craft a two-chamber Native American flute using clay. After all, Mesoamerican flute makers had extraordinary luck with clay, and I wanted to expand my ability and experience. Clay flutes have a distinctive sound that can be stereotypically called *haunting*. It's a sound immediately identifiable as Native American, but it differs somewhat from native flutes made of wood, bamboo, or plastic.

I began researching the topic on the internet, accessing numerous websites that contained general information about the history and use of clay for flutes. Most sites were devoid of specific information on crafting. One that contained information proved ridiculous, suggesting that the best way to form the basic tube for a flute is to roll clay around a long, inflated toy balloon. Instructions on other websites provided fewer how-to details but suggested air-dry ceramic and polymer clays would be a better choice than kiln-fired clays. A couple of videos on Youtube demonstrated selected steps in the process, but none provided complete instruction or addressed critical issues, such as insertion of the air plug, prevention of crumbling once the clay had dried, shaping air, sound, and finger holes, or the best method for finishing dried clay.

Utilizing the limited information available, I decided to experiment, to attempt to make a native flute with clay even though I had no experience working with the medium. I purchased air-dry clay, the instructions on the box assuring potential potters the clay would air-dry to a hard and durable material.

It didn't, as detailed in the following photographs.

Due to other commitments, orders, and life in general, that's as far as I've gotten with the clay experiment. Perhaps with a better clay product—maybe an air-dry polymer clay or a clay that must be kiln fired—the end product would be a playable flute rather than a crumbling waste of time. If you have experience in working with clay, espe-cially if you're handy with traditionally fired clay, then, by all means, craft a flute, utilizing your knowledge of the medium to shape the tube, form the holes, and insert the plug. For placement of finger holes and tuning, use the same percentages and formula provided in Chapter Eight. If you attempt this project successfully, please contact me. I'd love to feature your success through various social media.

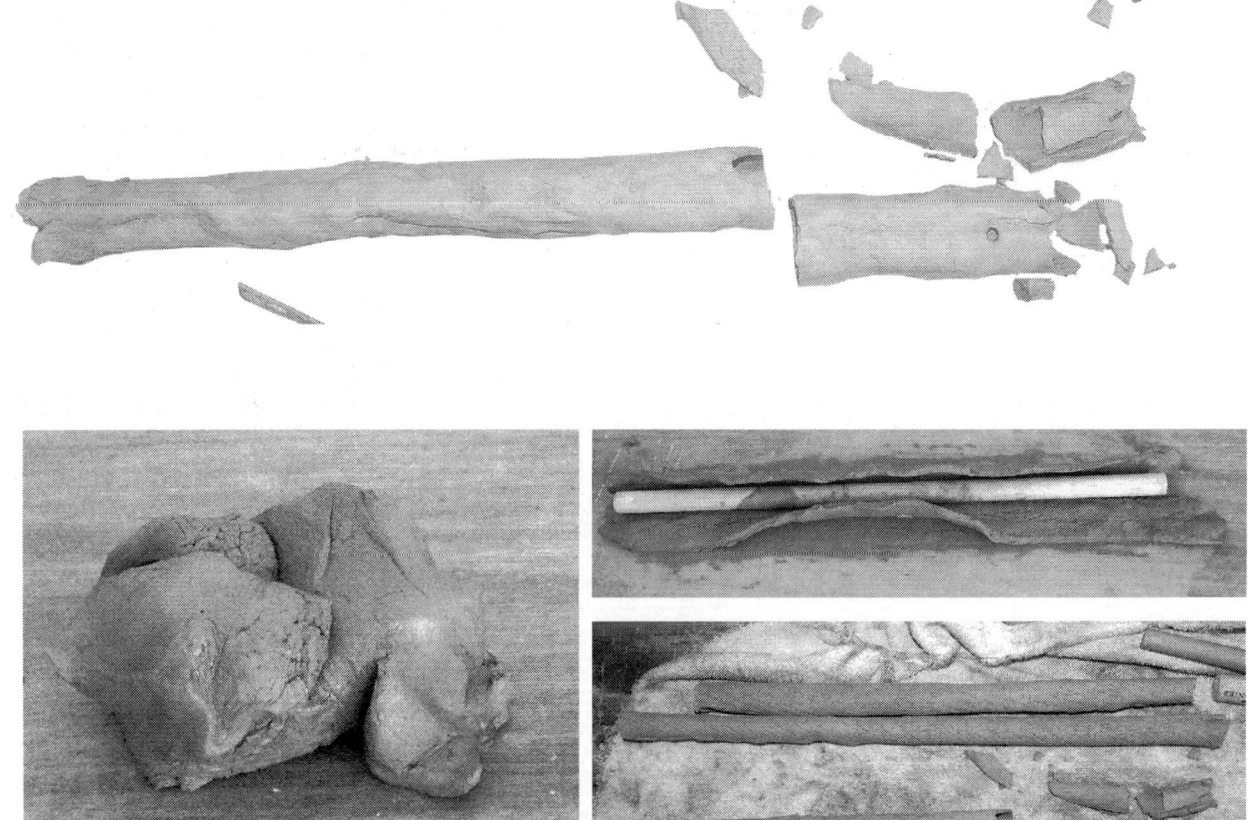

From the lump of air-dry clay on the left, I formed three tubes, each about 16 inches long, by rolling the flattened clay around a slightly dampened 3/4-inch dowel. After working the dowel gently out of each formed tube, I punched a screwdriver carefully through the damp clay to form the basic air and sound holes. Following manufacturer instructions, I allowed the clay to dry for more than 24 hours. As the clay dried, it became increasingly brittle. By the time it had fully dried, it could withstand very little pressure, breaking and crumbling easily, making it useless.

The Contrabass

A modern variation on the traditional Native American flute is now enjoying a spike in popularity. It's known as the Native American *contrabass* flute, an extraordinarily large flute that incorporates the pentatonic scale in a low octave, delivering resonant tones unattainable with conventional size Native American flutes. Be warned: Due to its large bore, huge finger holes, and long length, the contrabass flute is best suited for persons with extraordinarily wide hand reaches and large fingertip pads.

Crafters who offer this flute in wood employ various techniques to create the 1-1/2-inch or larger bore, primarily utilizing a wood lathe. Large bore bamboo is a good alternative to wood, but a mouthpiece will need to be fashioned since the open end of a large bore flute will probably be too big for the player's mouth to seal adequately. The best material for the first-time contrabass maker, in my opinion, is PVC. Large bore PVC pipe is readily and cheaply available. Mistakes, as described in the previous crafting chapters and depicted in the following photographs, are easily corrected with tape to allow the crafting of a playable flute while providing a template for future flutes.

The contrabass is usually crafted in the key of D, E, F#, or G. Although larger bores for flutes in standard keys can, in general, reduce the reach between finger holes, the large bores of the contrabass require, on average, a reach of more than an inch between each finger hole.

As the photos that follow detail, correcting mistakes on the first attempt can be accomplished with tape. I taped over incorrectly drilled holes, recalculated finger hole placement by decreasing the percentages, and drilled new holes. Although the first holes were tuned properly, the space between each hole proved too great for my ability. Finger hole diameter was also too large for my fingertips to cover adequately. However, even after adjusting placement, moving finger holes closer to the sound hole, the reach remained too great and the holes too large for me to play the instrument comfortably or effectively. If you have small hands or limited reach, the contrabass most likely will prove an unwise choice. An alternative exists, though. If you desire an instrument voiced lower than the standard Native American flute keys but with a workable reach, consider using a 1- to 1-1/2-inch diameter pipe (PVC, wood, or bamboo) to craft a C, C#, D, or Eb flute. Directions for a C# PVC flute are included in Chapter Eleven.

The contrabass will require a bird. Decide which you prefer—slide-on or standard tie-on—and utilize the instructions provided in Chapter Seven.

Materials

- 1-3/4 to 2-inch diameter PVC, at least 36-inches long
- matching size PVC pipe connector if using slide-on fetish
- matching size PVC knockout test cap or cork
- matching size PVC end cap
- fine, medium, coarse sandpaper
- cleanser
- fine grade steel wool
- spray lacquer or paint (optional)

Tools

- electronic chromatic tuner (a computer or smartphone application makes a great alternative to a stand-alone tuner)
- tape measure
- small handsaw
- straightedge at least 36 inches
- rotary tool
- 1/8-inch rotary tool drill bit
- flat and rounded needle files, no wider than 1/4-inch
- standard fine-tooth flat wood file
- sanding block
- sanding rod

Craft the Contrabass

1. Cut a 36-inch length of 1-3/4- to 2-inch diameter PVC pipe.

2. Approximately 3 inches from one end (this will be the mouthpiece end), use the rotary tool to drill a 1/8-inch air hole.

3. Approximately 1/2-inch to 3/4-inch from the air hole toward the foot end of the flute, drill the sound hole, making sure it is in line with the air hole.

4. Shape the sound and air holes into 1/4-inch squares, making certain that the holes are in-line. The air hole can be rounded rather than squared if preferred.

5. File the underside of sound hole's foot side to a roughly 45-degree angle, creating a blunt splitting edge 1/16 inch thick.

6. Cut or file off the knockout test cap's flange. If using cork, cut it to length to fit between sound and air holes.

7. Insert flange or cork into the pipe and slide it to a position between the air and sound holes.

8. Drill a 1/4-inch hole through the middle of the end cap. The end cap will serve as the mouthpiece when placed onto the head of the flute.

9. Craft the bird, utilizing the instructions provided in Chapter Seven.

10. Use the sanding block or wood file to flatten the barrel between the sound and air holes from 1/4-inch beyond each hole. Flatten enough to form the rectangular nest, about 3/16-inch wide.

11. Affix and test the fetish. Make adjustments as needed. Playing the contrabass requires better air control than the standard size Native American flute. It is easily overblown, producing shrill notes. If the sound is too airy, reduce the channel depth. If airflow is restricted, increase the depth. Make sure the fetish is seated properly over the air and labium holes. If no note is

produced, check the labium for uniformity and anomalies. You may have to experiment.

12. Bring the fundamental/key note to desired pitch by shortening the flute's foot end incrementally, cutting no more than 1/4-inch off at a time, testing the note after each cut.

13. Use the straightedge to draw a line from the middle of the sound hole to the foot end as a guide for uniform placement of finger holes. Consider placing finger holes 1 and 2 right of center and holes 4 and 5 left of center in the same manner as finger hole placement for the Anasazi flute. Off-center placement can improve reach.

14. Using the following percentages and formula to determine placement of finger holes.

> Sound Chamber Length (from sound hole to foot) x Percentage = Hole Placement

Placement percentages may need slight adjustment since these will result in extreme distances between large finger holes. However, even when percentages are adjusted, the resulting space between finger holes remains considerable and the size of the finger hole remains large.

- hole 1, 64.5 percent measuring from sound hole center
- hole 2, 58 percent
- hole 3, 51 percent
- hole 4, 44 percent
- hole 5, 38 percent
- hole 6, 31 percent

15. Enlarge each hole incrementally to desired pitch before proceeding to the next hole.

16. After completing the notes, use fine-grade sandpaper to remove remnants from holes.

17. Use the sanding rod to remove remnants from barrel interior.

18. Use the cleanser and fine grade steel wool to remove factory-applied lettering from the flute's exterior.

19. If desired, finish the flute with lacquer or paint and allow 24 hours to dry.

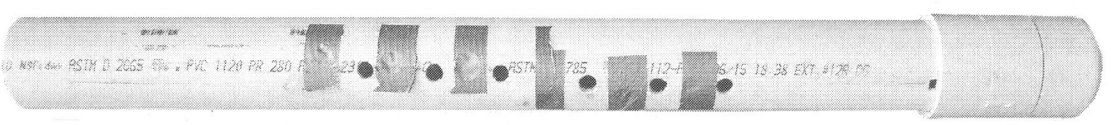

Craft the PVC Contrabass Illustrated

End cap, connector, cork, and knockout plug.

Mark and drill sound and air holes.

Slide plug or cork into barrel between air and sound holes.

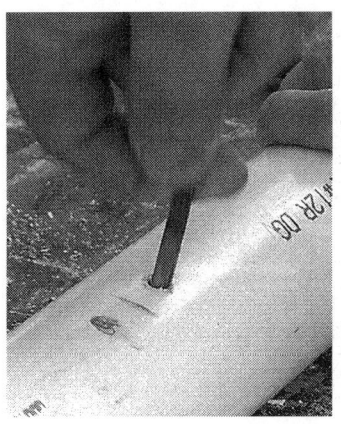

Shape sound and air holes.

Drill end-cap mouthpiece hole.

Flatten nest and affix bird.

Shorten to desired fundamental and drill and tune finger holes.

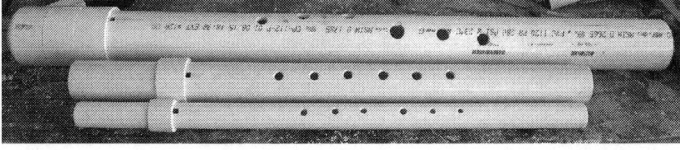

Above, the contrabass is pictured with a C# and an E flute. The C# (crafting instructions in Chapter Eleven) is an easy-to-play, low-key flute. (Below) The contrabass was too big to play comfortably, even when corrected.

Chapter Thirteen

Correcting Problems & Mistakes

No matter how adept a flute maker, mistakes will happen. It's inevitable, the one universal law you can bank on. In my experience, the crafting of Native American flutes has proved part technical ability, part artistic ability, mixed with a good helping of intuition and luck. It's a folk craft that hasn't been overly polluted by mass production that turns out a billion exact copies each day—yet. And that means each flute has advantages and flaws. As a folk crafter, you'll make mistakes no matter how talented, no matter how technically gifted you are. An incorrectly placed finger hole, a sound hole drilled too large, a channel too shallow or too deep—some kind of slip will bless you with irritation. The worst mistake is the kind that can't be corrected. Luckily, many of the mistakes a crafter makes with a Native American flute *can* be corrected, even though the correction might not be *pretty*.

Flute kits can prove to be a good learning tool for a new crafter. Many of the mistakes that will be encountered at some point are built-in with some kits. Kits are offered with the flute in various stages of completion, enabling a novice crafter to craft his/her instrument in some measure while learning the process. Most kits, if not all, come with air, sound, and finger holes pre-drilled, the flute—even though it's never been assembled—supposedly pre-tuned. While the basic location of holes may be the same if flute parts are crafted by machines spitting out replica after replica, they still require fine tuning after the flute is assembled. Small variations in the fetish, sound hole, or finger holes can render notes either sharp or flat. If a note's flat, it can usually be corrected by incremental enlargement of the finger hole. If a pre-drilled hole is sharp, however, the crafter has two choices—tune the flute's fundamental note and all finger notes sharp to match the existing sharp note, making the flute in tune with itself, or employ the following remedy.

Correct Hole Mistakes

If a finger hole renders a note sharp, or if a hole cannot be enlarged enough to sharpen to the target note, the crafter has a ready remedy available. These instructions can also be used to correct faulty air and sound holes.

Materials and Tools

- electric drill
- drill bit, size determined by hole requirement
- carpenter's glue
- wood dowel, size determined by drill bit
- fine-tooth saw
- sandpaper
- sanding rod

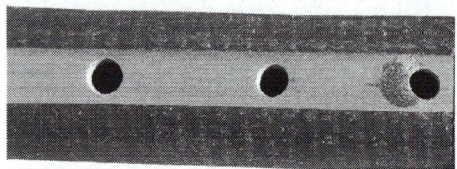

In the above photo, the hole on the right has been repaired with a dowel. The area is masked with tape for painting. The bottom photo demonstrates how paint hides the repair.

1. Enlarge the faulty hole to the next size wood dowel diameter.

2. Coat the dowel tip's sides with glue.

3. Insert the dowel end into the hole without protruding beyond the interior wall.

4. Allow the glue to dry.

5. Cut the dowel flush with the flute exterior.

6. Sand the area smooth.

7. Use the sanding rod to sand smooth the repaired area inside the barrel.

8. Calculate and drill the new hole, based on the experience with the faulty hole. If the original hole would not sharpen enough through enlargement, place the new hole more toward the sound hole. If the original hole was already sharp, place the new location more toward the foot of the flute.

Correct Air Leaks

If an air leak occurs along a wooden flute's seam, run a bead of wood glue along the seam where air's escaping. Carefully force the glue into the seam by *smoothing* it in with your finger. Clamp and allow to dry for 24 hours

If an air leak occurs around the interior plug between the air chamber and sound chamber, the plug can be replaced easily if it's cork or patched with wood putty if it's wood.

Repair a Wood Plug

1. Apply a small amount of wood putty to the flat end of a dowel that's slightly smaller in diameter than the flute bore.

2. Slide the putty-tipped dowel down the barrel to the plug.

3. Gently work the putty into spaces where the leak may be occurring.

4. Repeat the process several times to ensure material is packed well into areas that may be leaking.

5. Allow to dry.

6. With the homemade sanding rod, remove any putty remnants from the flute barrel interior.

7. Clean the flute's interior in accordance with the flute's finish.

Replace a Plug

1. Drill out the old plug with an extra-long drill bit that's slightly smaller than the flute bore.

2. After drilling out the plug, use the sanding rod to smooth the interior bore between the air and sound holes.

3. Fashion a new plug that fits tightly into the flute bore. I prefer cork for its flexibility.

4. Use a long wooden dowel with a diameter slightly smaller than the flute bore to slide the plug down the barrel and into place between the two chambers.

Correct a Sharp Key

If you want an F# flute but cut the flute barrel so short that it's fundamental note is G, must you settle, or discard the flute and start over? Neither.

One of my favorite flutes is crafted from bamboo. I wanted to craft an E flute with this particular piece of bamboo, but I cut it too short, and the initial fundamental note was an F. I don't particularly like the key of F, so I had a choice. I could either cut the flute shorter to make it an F# or G, or I could *extend* it to the key of E.

I cut a short length of PVC that had a slightly larger diameter than the flute's interior bore. Using a flat file and sandpaper, I decreased the exterior diameter of the PVC piece just enough to fit it snugly into the flute's bore. Secured with glue, the PVC lengthened the flute some two inches. I then shortened the extension to attain the desired E fundamental. This flute, with a clear, strong voice, is still the one I most often play.

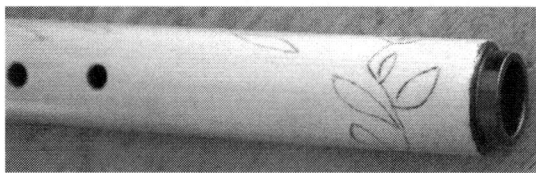

Using a short length of PVC pipe, the flute's sound chamber could be extended, lowering the fundamental note to the desired pitch.

Adjust Air Channel

It's unlikely the flute will sound perfect the first time you blow it. It'll likely be too airy, too soft in volume, or simply unable to produce a satisfactory note, perhaps nothing at all. The problem in these cases usually stems from anomalies with the channel and/or the sound hole's splitting edge. If the sound hole is the problem and cannot be corrected by better shaping the splitting edge, then hole correction as detailed above may be necessary. If the problem stems from a faulty channel, a few steps can be taken for correction.

If the channel is carved into the body of the flute and it's too shallow to allow proper airflow to produce a note, then deepen the channel slightly. If, however, the channel is so deep it creates an extremely airy sound or directs air improperly across the labium to produce no note at all, then the flute's nest must be sanded to decrease the channel depth. Sanding the nest can be tricky and potentially fatal to the flute. It's easy to sand too much, ruining the flute altogether—the primary reason I prefer carving the channel into the bottom of the bird. When adjusting the nest channel, use a sanding block and uniform pressure to ensure even sanding and uniform channel depth. If channel depth varies in different locations, air will not be properly directed to the labium, requiring even for more corrective action.

If the channel is carved into the bottom of the fetish, adjustment is not as critical as channel adjustment to a flute's nest. Even if you decrease channel depth too much, a new channel can be carved. If you destroy the bird completely, it's easily replaced with another.

In general, to decrease airiness and focus airflow more directly, decrease the channel's depth. To increase airflow, deepen the channel.

Most crafters maintain that the channel, especially when it's part of the fetish, must be flat and uniform from back to front. In my experience, a flute's sound has sometimes improved when I've deepened the channel slightly more in the back of the fetish (the part that sits over the air hole), sloping it to a shallower depth at the front. However, a flat, smooth channel generally produces the desired sound.

No *fix* will work in every situation on every flute. A crafter must experiment to achieve the best sound. The results aren't always those desired, but each experiment and each adjustment is a learning experience that improves the crafter's ability. Eventually, with a simple channel adjustment or a new fetish altogether, the desired sound can usually be achieved.

Moisture

Moisture condensation from the player's breath can prove a regular irritation, especially when it accumulates in the channel enough to stop sound completely—inevitably in the middle of a performance. Further, moisture condensation, even when it doesn't hinder sound while playing, can result in later problems by creating residue as it dries, residue that accumulates over time to degrade sound quality incrementally.

To prevent such problems, slide off the fetish between songs and dry the nest and channel with a soft cloth, such as a cotton diaper. Dry the areas again upon completion of playing.

If the flute has a closed air chamber

with access through only the small mouthpiece hole, store the flute vertically with the mouthpiece down, enabling moisture to drain out of the flute.

Suddenly Sharp or Flat

If a bird is not seated properly, it can result in several problems, including excessive airiness, degradation in sound and volume, and the sudden change in notes to play sharp or flat.

Usually, simply adjusting the bird slightly toward or away from the sound hole can improve pitch and sound quality.

Clean the channel and barrel often to ensure the best sound quality possible. During performances, check the bird between songs to ensure it's properly seated at the sound hole's mouthpiece edge.

Decoration

Some crafters contend that decorations such as ties, leather straps, beads, and other native-type paraphernalia adversely affect a flute's sound quality. I have not encountered that problem, but I don't decorate my flutes excessively. At most, I paint the flutes and secure fetishes with leather ties that are sometimes decorated with beads.

Decoration should be left to the flute owner's whim. Beads, feathers, and leather ties are the most common decorations, along with images that are burned or painted on the flute body. Perhaps the best rule of thumb is not to overdo it. After all, you don't want the flute's appearance to draw more attention than the beauty of its sound. What matters most is that you're happy with the instrument. Perhaps my uncle said it best: "Whatever toots your flute."

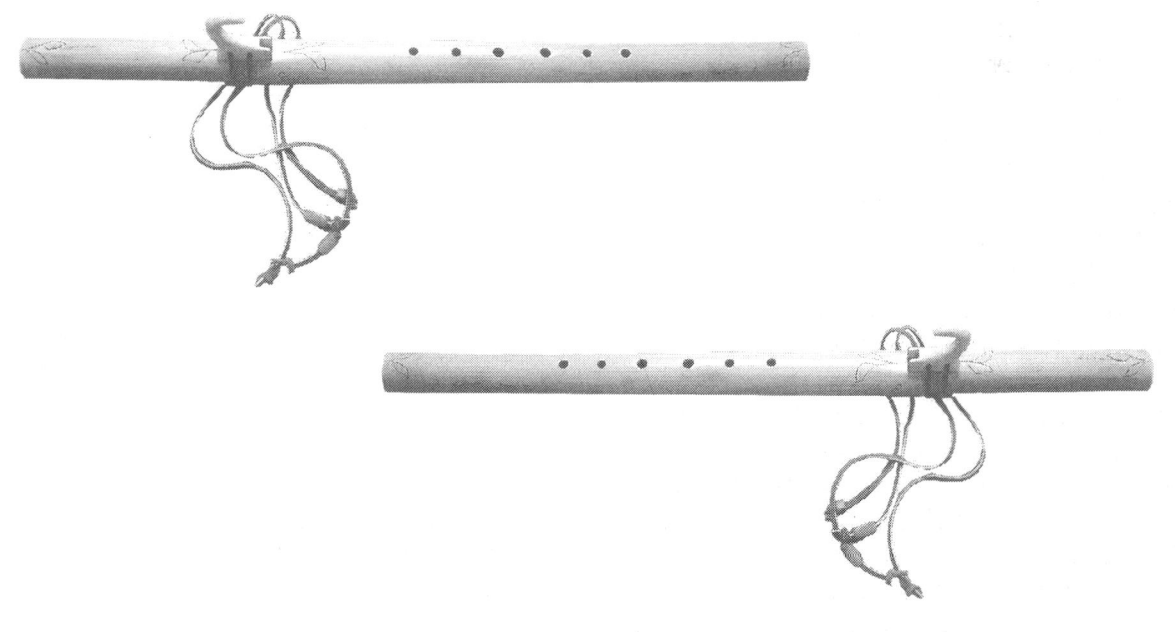

Chapter Fourteen

Sources

Flute Makers

The internet was in its infancy when I began to craft Native American flutes, and the art of flute-making wasn't as widespread as it is today. Locating competent flute makers proved a difficult task. That's no longer the case. Hundreds of flute makers—some seasoned, some novice—advertise via the internet and are located in many countries. You can use internet search engines to locate crafters of all levels, and a few databases listing many are also available. The following databases catalog primarily U.S.-based crafters, though Native American flutes are made by crafters from around the world. Along with the databases, I've included links to a few flute makers in the U.K., New Zealand, and Australia.

The crafters here are provided without endorsement. I have little or no direct knowledge of these crafters or their work beyond what's provided on their respective websites. The only craftsperson I can endorse from personal experience is Michael Graham Allen, founder of Coyote Oldman. His flutes are immaculate, built with care, experience, and unrivaled technical and aesthetic perfection.

Individual Crafters

- Coyote Oldman Flutes, Michael Graham Allen, United States
  http://coyoteoldman.com/

- Southern Cross Flutes, Todd Chaplin, New Zealand
  http://www.southerncrossflutes.com

- Earthsongs Flutes, Australia
  http://www.earthsongflutes.com.au

❧ Spirit Winds Flutes, Tony Richards, Australia
http://www.spiritwinds.com.au

Crafter Databases

United Kingdom:
❧ http://www.nativeflutes.org.uk/

United States:
❧ http://www.littleleaf.com/flutemakers.htm

❧ http://www.worldflutes.org/flute_makers/

❧ http://www.wakingspiritflutes.com/List-of-Flute-Makers.html

❧ http://www.flutetree.com/links/Makers.html

Bamboo Suppliers

The following list is only a sampling of bamboo suppliers. Before ordering from any vendor, explore its offerings and references. No endorsement of the following suppliers is intended or implied.

❧ Bamboo & Koi Garden, Bamboo Company Nursery LLC, Franklinton, LA
http://www.moso.us/

❧ Bamboo Gardens, North Plains, OR
http://www.bamboogarden.com/

❧ Bamboo Giant, Aptos, CA
http://www.bamboogiant.com

❧ Bamboo Habitat, Perkiomenville, PA
http://www.bamboohabitat.com

❧ The Bamboo Man, Miami, FL
http://www.bambooman.net

❧ BS Bamboo Supplies, United Kingdom
www.bs-bamboo.co.uk

❧ Cali Bamboo, San Diego, CA
http://www.calibamboo.com

❧ Frank's Cane and Rush Supply, Huntington Beach, CA
http://www.franksupply.com/

❧ Haiku Bamboo Nursery, Edneyville, NC
http://www.haikubamboonursery.net

❧ Jade Mountain Bamboo Nursery, Tacoma, WA
http://www.jademountainnursery.com/

❧ Lewis Bamboo, Inc., Oakman, AL
http://www.lewisbamboo.com

❧ Ozark Bamboo Garden, Eureka Springs, AR
http://www.ozarkbamboogarden.com/

❧ Tradewinds Bamboo Nursery, Gold Beach, OR,

http://www.bamboodirect.com/

➤ UK Bamboo Supplies Limited, United Kingdom
http://www.ukbamboo.com

Aromatic Cedar Suppliers

No endorsement of the following suppliers is intended or implied.

➤ Capitol City Lumber Raleigh, NC
http://www.capitolcitylumber.com/lumber-plywood/cedar/aromatic-cedar

➤ Cedar Specialties, Medford, NJ
http://www.cedarspecialties.com

➤ Hearne Hardwoods Inc., Oxford PA
http://www.hearnehardwoods.com

➤ Mitchell Hollow Wood Products, Doniphan, MO
https://www.cedar-closet-linings.com

➤ Woodworkers Source, **Tempe**, AZ
http://www.woodworkerssource.com

Sheet Music Sources

PlayFolkInstruments.com is operated by Dick Claassen, author, instructor, and Native American flute musician. Dick operates one of the best resources for Native American flute instructional and sheet music books available. No endorsement of any other source listed here is intended or implied.

➤ PlayFolkInstruments.com offers numerous music tab books for NAF flute, from gospel hymns to blues to traditional Native American tunes. For more information about these books and instruction packages, visit http://www.PlayFolkInstruments.com.

➤ Flutetree.com maintains several songbooks for Native American flute, including a songbook for contemporary Native American flute.
http://www.flutetree.com/songbook/contemporary/index.html

➤ The Yahoo group NAF Music provides free Native American flute sheet music to members.
https://groups.yahoo.com/neo/groups/NAFMusic/info

➤ Flutetree.com provides a listing of songbooks and other tablature on the web.
http://www.flutetree.com/songbook/web

➤ Laughing Crow Flutes has a

selection of songbooks by artists such as Mary Youngblood.
http://cedarflutes.com/Native_American_Flute_Songbooks_CDs.htm

Cork Suppliers

No endorsement is intended or implied by the following list. Local suppliers, such as wine and beer making shops, department stores, hobby stores, and national building supply stores, stock cork stoppers, particularly those used in wine bottles, which are perfect for 3/4-inch diameter flutes. The following are online suppliers.

- Jelinek Cork Group
  http://www.corkstore.com/Products/Closures-Stoppers

- Manton Cork
  http://www.mantoncork.com/

- Bangor Cork
  http://www.bangorcork.com/

- Widgetco, Inc.
  http://www.widgetco.com/cork-stoppers

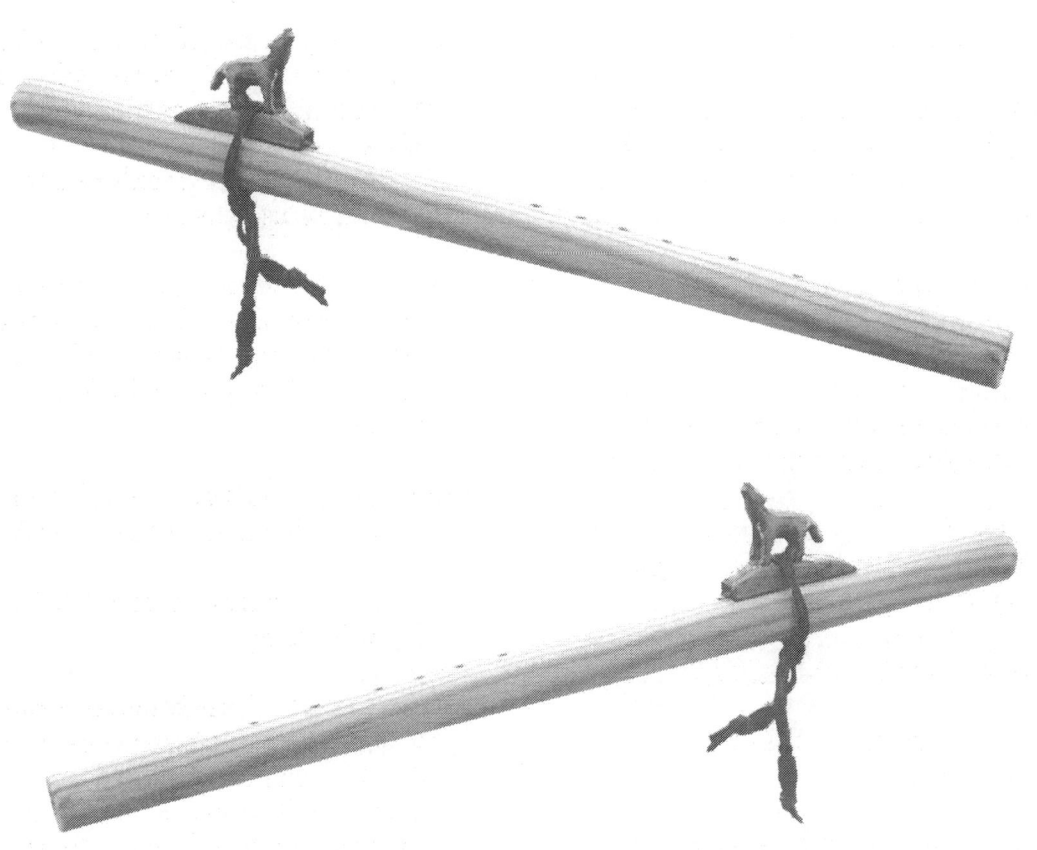

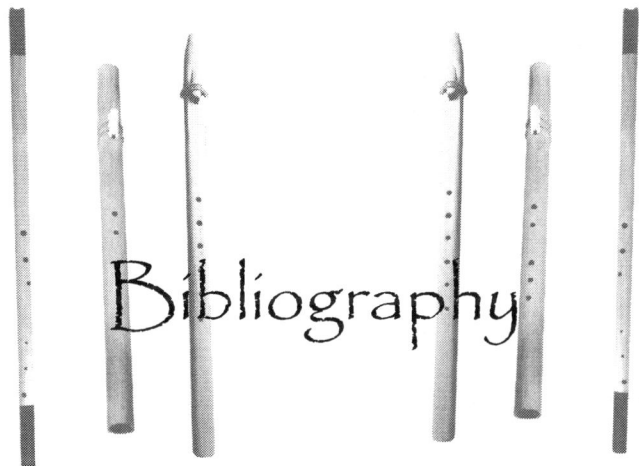

Bibliography

"About Rivercane." About Rivercane. Mississippi State University. Web. 28 Mar. 2015. <http://www.rivercane.msstate.edu/about/>.

"About Zuni Fetishes - American Indian Art / Fetish Meanings." *About Zuni Fetishes - American Indian Art / Fetish Meanings*. Zunifetishstore.com. Web. 6 Apr. 2015. <http://www.zunifetishstore.com/?view=about-zuni-fetish>.

Allen, Paula Gunn. *Grandmothers of the Light: A Medicine Woman's Sourcebook*. Boston, MA: Beacon Press, 1991.

---. *The Sacred Hoop : Recovering the Feminine in American Indian Traditions*. Boston, MA: Beacon Press, 1992.

The Anasazi. Desert USA. 2007. January 2007. <http://www.desertusa.com/ind1/du_peo_ana.html>.

Ancestral Puebloans. The People of the Colorado Plateau. January 2007. <http://www.4corners.net/ccyc/text5.html>.

"Arizona Museum of Natural History." Mesoamerica. Arizona Museum of Natural History, n.d. Web. 27 Apr. 2015. http://azmnh.org/exhibits/cultures/mesoamerica.aspx>.

Arnold, Caroline. *The Ancient Cliff Dwellers of Mesa Verde: A Close Look at the Anasazi*. New York: Clarion Books, a Houghton Mifflin Company, 1992.

August, Scott. *About the Native American Flute*. Cedar Mesa Music. 2005. January 2007. <http://cedarmesa.com/flutehistory.html#History>.

August, Scott. "The Mojave Flute." *The Mojave Flute*. Cedar Mesa Music. Web. March 2015. <http://www.cedarmesa.com/blogfiles/mojaveflute/mojaveflute.html>.

The Bamboo Flute. Historical Folk Toys, LLC. 2004-2006. <http://www.historicalfolktoys.com/catcont/5003.html>.

Bertola, Max. *Kokopelli: Anasazi Casanova*. Max Bertola's Southern Utah. 1996. January 2007. <http://www.so-utah.com/feature/kokopeli/homepage.html>.

Boyle, Alan. *Listening to the sounds of science: Researchers make music from ancient flutes, saws and flames*. MSNBC Interactive. February 21, 2000. January 2007. <http://www.msnbc.msn.com/id/3077403/>.

A Brief Native American Flute History. Wild Horse Mountain Flutes. January 2007. <http://www.wildhorsemtnflutes.com/>.

Bruchac, Marge. *Reclaiming the Word "Squaw" in the Name of the Ancestors*. NativeWeb.org. November 1999. <http://www.nativeweb.org/pages/legal/squaw.html>.

Carrington, Damian. *Oldest flute sounds again*. BBC January 2007. News Online. February 2, 2000. <http://news.bbc.co.uk/1/hi/sci/tech/specials/washington_2000/649296.stm>.

Claassen, Dick. *Celebrate the Native American Flute*. Iowa: Awe-Struck E-Books, Inc., 2004. <http://www.awe-struck.net/NONFICTION2/cnaf.html>.

Crawford, Mark. "From Flutes to Fenders: Today's Native American Music." *News From Indian Country*. May 15, 1997.

Crow, Joseph Medicine. *From the Hear of Crow Country—The Crow Indians' Own Story*. New York: Orion Books, a Division of Crown Publishers, Inc., 1992.

"CVPA Health & Safety Manual-studios." *CVPA Health & Safety Manual-studios*. University of Massachusetts, Dartmouth, n.d. Web. 29 Mar. 2015. <http://www1.umassd.edu/cvpa/safety/ceramics.html>.

Diamon, Jared. *Collapse: How Societies Choose to Fail or Succeed*. New York: Penguin Books, 2006.

Doc Tate Nevaquaya: Comanche Flute. Smithsonian Global Sound. 2007. January 2007. <http://www.smithsonianglobalsound.org/containerdetail.aspx?itemid=3025>.

"Double Flute/Drone Flute." Double Flute, Drone Flute Photos, Maps, Videos, History. Native Flutes Walking, n.d. Web. 27 Apr. 2015. <http://www.nativefluteswalking.com/double-flute-drone-flute.shtml>.

Doyle, Martin. "Martin Doyle Flutes." *Woods Used For Making Flutes*. Martin Doyle Flutes, n.d. Web. 28 Mar. 2015. <http://www.martindoyleflutes.com/woods.html>.

Dunn, Adam. *Did the Chinese discover America? New book asserts a different version of history*. Cable News Network. January 13, 2003. January

2007. <http://www5.cnn.com/2003/SHOWBIZ/books/01/13/1421>.

Eller, Cynthia. *The Myth of Matriarchal Prehistory: Why an Invented Past Won't Give Women a Future.* Boston, MA: Beacon Press, 2000.

Ench, Rick and Jay Cravath. *North American Indian Music.* New York: Franklin Watts, a Division of Scholastic Inc., 2002.

Erdoes, Richard and Alfonso Ortiz. *American Indian Myths and Legends.* New York: Pantheon Books, 1984.

Farrelly, David. *The Book of Bamboo: A comprehensive Guide to this Remarkable Plant, Its Uses, and Its History.* San Francisco, CA: Sierra Club Books, 1984.

Fauntleroy, Gussie. "Timeless Native American Instruments." *Native Peoples.* November/December 2006: p. 29-32.

"Fetishism." Www.warpaths2peacepipes.com. Web. 6 Apr. 2015. <http://www.warpaths2peacepipes.com/native-american-culture/fetishism.htm>.

The Four Corners Area. Talking Stones Tours. January 14, 2007. <http://www.talkingstoneshikingtours.com/historical%20information.htm>.

Fretwell, Jerry & Lisa. "Native American Flute Fingering Charts - Tabs - 5 Hole Flute - 6 Hole Flute." *Native American Flute Fingering Charts - Tabs - 5 Hole Flute - 6 Hole Flute.* Web. 19 Mar. 2015. <http://www.fretwellflutes.com/FingeringCharts.html>.

Gatliff, Robert. *Early written accounts of the native flutes from 1528-1869 in North America.* FluteTree.com. May 8, 2006. <http://www.flutetree.com/nature/EarlyWrittenAccounts.html>.

Goss, Clint. *Anasazi Flutes from the Broken Flute Cave.* FluteKey.com. Web. February 19, 2007. <http://www.flutekey.com/htm/brokenflutecave.htm>.

---. "Flute Binding." *Clintgoss.com.* Clint Goss. Web. 1 Apr. 2015. <http://clintgoss.com/binding.html>.

Gromicko, Nick. "PVC Health Hazards." - *Int'l Association of Certified Home Inspectors (InterNACHI).* International Association of Certified Home Inspectors, Inc., n.d. Web. 29 Mar. 2015. <http://www.nachi.org/pvc-health-hazards.htm>.

Harjo, Suzan Shown. *Respect Native Women—Stop Using the S-Word.* Indian Country Today. February 28, 2001. January 2007. <http://indiancountry.com/content.cfm?id=2704>.

Heslet, Lars. *Our Musical Brain.* in:fusion— Kongress in Salzburg. 2005. January 2007. <http://www.infusion.at/Nachlese/dokumentationen/musichumana.html>.

History of Pueblo Indians. Pueblo Indian. October 17, 2002. January 2007. <http://www.puebloindian.com/>.

The History of the Hopi Flute Ceremony. Brownielocks and the Three Bears. 1999-2007. January 2007. <http://www.brownielocks.com/fluteceremony.html>.

History of the Native American Flute. Falcon Flutes and Drums January 2007. <http://www.falconflutes.com/History%20of%20the%20Native%20American%20Flute.htm>.

Hofsinde, Robert. *Indian Music Makers.* New York: William Morrow Company, Inc., 1967.

In Beauty I Walk. Watford, Hertfordshire, UK & Spencer, MA: Exley Publications, 1997.

The Indians. New York: Time-Life Books, 1973.

Jacobson, Paul. "Humidity & Your Guitar's Health." *Hand Crafted Guitars.* Pjguitar.com. Web. 1 Apr. 2015. <http://www.pjguitar.com/articles/humidity-guitars-health/>.

Jewitt, Jeff. "Selecting a Finish." FineWoodworking.com. FineWoodworking.com. Web. 30 Mar. 2015. <http://www.finewoodworking.com/toolguide/articles/selecting-a-finish.aspx>.

Karnowski, Steve, "Archaeologists find ancient stone tools." *Associated Press.* January 12, 2007.

Krakovsky, Marina. *Dubious 'Mozart Effect' remains music to many Americans'* ears. Stanford Report. February 2, 2005. January 2007. <http://news-service.stanford.edu/news/2005/february2/mozart-020205.html>.

King, Tom. "Howdy Ya Dewit!" : Selecting Wood for Your Musical Instrument Project. Tom King, 8 Aug. 2010. Web. 28 Mar. 2015. <http://howdyyadewit.blogspot.com/2010/08/selecting-wood-for-your-musical.html#.VRb8omYVtq1>.

Lame Deer, John (Fire) and Richard Erdoes. *Lame Deer, Seeker of Visions, Revised Edition.* New York: Washington Square Press of Pocket Books, 1994.

Lander, Nicholas S. *Instrument of Torture or Instrument of Music?* Recorder Home Page. January 11, 2007. <http://www.recorderhomepage.net/torture2.html>.

Lorenzi, Rossella. *Flute Dates Origins of Music to Ice Age.* Discovery News. December 28, 2004. January 2007. <http://www.urgeschichte.uni-tuebing-en.de/fileadmin/downloads/Medien/Flute/DiscoveryChannelFlute.pdf>.

"Maintaining Your Instrument." Woodenflute.com. Woodenflute.com. Web. 30 Mar. 2015. <http://www.woodenflute.com/maintaining>.

Manitou Cliff Dwellings. Manitou Cliff Dwellings Museum. June 11, 2004. January 2007. <http://www.cliffdwellingsmuseu

m.com/default.asp>.

Menzies, Gavin. *1421: The Year China Discovered America.* 1421 Team. November 2002 to present. <http://www.1421.tv/> January 2007.

Mozart Effect Lesson Plan. Science NetLinks. September 20, 2001. January 2007. <http://www.sciencenetlinks.com/Lessons.cfm?DocID=36>.

Musical Instruments of the World, An Illustrated Encyclopedia. New York: Diagram Group, 1976.

Nakai, R. Carlos and James DeMar. *The Art of the Native American Flute.* Phoenix, AZ: Canyon Records Productions, 1996.

Native American Creation Myths. Crystalinks. 2007. January 2007. <http://www.crystalinks.com/nativeamcreation.html>.

Native American Creation Myths: Creation By Women. Crystalinks. 2007. January 2007. <http://www.crystalinks.com/namcreationwomen.html>.

The Native American Flute. Ancestral Engineering. 2007. January 2007. <http://nativeaccess.com/ancestral/flutes-1.html>.

Native American Flute Heritage and History. Heritage Ethnic Music Online. January 2007. <http://www.heritageethnicmusic.com/site/607029/page/272397>.

Native American Wisdom. Philadelphia, PA: Running Press, 1993.

Native Flutes. Indians.org. 2006. January 2007. <http://www.indians.org/articles/native-american-flute.html>.

"Native Flutes of Mesoamerica." Mesoamerican Native Flute Photos, Maps, Videos, History. Native Flutes Walking, n.d. Web. 28 Mar. 2015. <http://www.nativefluteswalking.com/native-flutes-mesoamerica.shtml>.

The Neanderthal flute. Answers.com. November 2006. January 2007. <http://www.answers.com/topic/divje-babe>.

Neanderthal jam. The Why Files, University of Wisconsin. 2000. January 2007. <http://whyfiles.org/114music/4.html>.

Neihardt, John G. *Black Elk Speaks.* New York: MJF Books, 1932.

"Ocarina." Tips. Www.okarina-information.com. Web. 1 Apr. 2015. <http://www.ocarina-information.com/articles/54-ocarina-tips.htm>.

Oliver, Rob. *Can Music Heal?* Healing Singing Website. January 2007. <http://www.healingsinging.com/can_music_heal.htm>.

Paige, Joseph. *History of the Native American Flute.* Native Languages of the Americas. 2006. January 2007. <http://www.native-languages.org/composition/native-american-flute-2.html>.

Pecos Classification. Pueblo Indian. April 19, 2002. January 2007. <http://www.puebloindian.com/pecos_classification.htm>.

Pentatonic Flute Scale Pictorial. FluteSpirit.com. <http://www.flutespirit.com/PrivateLesson/Dvorak/FluteScale.html> January 2007.

"Pre-Boehm" or Early Flutes: The development of the flute—80,000 BC to 1878 AD.   January   2007. <http://www.jinyinusa.com/BPMflutehist.htm>.

Polak, Simon. "Simon Polak: Early Flutes." *Woods*. Simon Polak, n.d. Web. 28 Mar. 2015. <http://www.earlyflute.com/earlyflutenew7/pages/flutewoods.html>.

Powers, Wendy. *The Development of the Recorder*. The Metropolitan Museum of Art. 2000. January 2007. <http://www.metmuseum.org/toah/hd/recd/hd_recd.htm>.

"Pre-Columbian Music of Mesoamerica." Encyclopedia of Latin American History and Culture. 2008. Encyclopedia.com. 27 Apr. 2015 <http://www.encyclopedia.com>.

Presutti, Michael. "The Pros and Cons of Lacquers and Polyurethane." Silive.com. Silive.com, 22 July 2009. Web. 30 Mar. 2015. <http://www.silive.com/homegarden/homeimprovement/index.ssf/2009/07/the_pros_and_cons_of_lacquers.html>.

Price, Lew Paxton. *Creating and Using the Native American Love Flute*. Garden Valley, California: Lew Paxton Price, 1994.

---. *Creating and Using Grandfather's Flute*. Garden Valley, California: Lew Paxton Price, 1995.

Rasmussen, Ray. *The Anasazi and Kokopelli*. Ray's Web. January 2007. <http://raysweb.net/canyonlands/pages/anasazi.html>.

Richard Payne biographical information. Douglas Spotted Eagle. January 2007. <http://www.spottedeagle.com/toubat.htm>.

Schneider, Achim. *Ice-age musicians fashioned ivory flute*. Nature. December 17,   2004 <http://www.urgeschichte.uni-tuebingen.de/fileadmin/downloads/Medien/Flute/nature.pdf> January 2007.

A Short History of the Flute." A Short History of the Modern Flute. Serenity Bamboo Flutes, n.d. Web. 28 Mar. 2015. <http://www.serenitybambooflutes.com/flute-history.html>.

The Spirit World. Alexandria, VA: Time-Life Books, 1992.

Spotted Eagle, Douglas. Douglas Spotted Eagle. 2007. January 2007. <http://www.spottedeagle.com/flutes.htm>.

Stillwell, John Stillwell. "Finish Materials for the Native American Style Flute." Ancient Territories. John

Stillwell. Web. 30 Mar. 2015. <http://www.atflutes.com/native-american-style-flute-finishes/flutes/making-flutes/flute-finishes>.

—. "Tuning of the Native American Style Flute." *Flute Tuning*. Web. 19 Mar. 2015. <http://www.atflutes.com/native-american-style-flute-tuning/flutes/learning-the-flute/flute-tuning>.

Teal, Kim J. *Flute Facts and Fun Page*. 2007. March 2007. <http://members.glis.net/kjt/tealflutestudio/FluteFacts&Fun.html>.

Torson, Dianna, "Communication and the Power of the Native American Women." Master's Thesis, South Dakota State University. 1990.

Turner, Sarah E. "Spider Woman's Granddaughter: Autobiographical Writings by Native American Women." *MELUS*. Volume 22. No. 4, Winter 1997: p 109-132.

Two-Hawks, John. John Two-Hawks, composer. January 2007. <http://www.johntwohawks.com>.

Wagner, Sally Roesch. *The Untold Story of the Iroquois Influence on Early Feminists*. Aberdeen, SD: Sky Carrier Press, 1996.

Wahpeconiah, Edward Wapp. *The American Indian Courting Flute: Revitalization and Change*. Mississippi State University. January 2007. <http://www.msstate.edu/fineart_online/Gallery/Trophies/wapp.htm>.

Wegst, Ulrike G. K. Wegst2. "American Journal of Botany." Wood for Sound. American Journal of Botany, 17 July 2006. Web. 28 Mar. 2015. <http://www.amjbot.org/content/93/10/1439.full>.

"What Is a Fetish?-Native American Art and Images." Grandfathersspirit.com. Web. 6 Apr. 2015. <http://www.grandfathersspirit.com/What-is-a-Fetish.html>.

White Buffalo Calf Woman and the Mother of Life. Goddess Gift. 2006. January 2007. <http://www.goddessgift.com/goddess-myths/white_buffalo_calf_woman.htm>.

White Buffalo Calf Woman Brings the First Pipe, as told by John Fire Lame Deer in 1967. Native American Resources. June 25, 1996. January 2007. <http://www.kstrom.net/isk/arvol/lamedeer.html>.

White, Julia. *Looking Back*. Innerspace. 2007. January 2007. <http://www.meyna.com/lookback.html>.

Wood Finishes and Stains." *WOOD FINISHES AND STAINS* (2005): 1-8. *Wood Finishes and Stains*. Choose Green Report, Feb. 2005. Web. 30 Mar. 2015. <https://www.wbdg.org/ccb/GREEN/REPORTS/cgrwoodfinish.pdf>.

Yasaitis, Kelly E. *Gender Issues, Transaction Publishers, Native American Women: Where Are They Today? Gender Issues*. No. 4, vol. 21, 2003: p. 71-80.

C.S. Fuqua has worked as a newspaper reporter, magazine editor, book editor, English tutor, substitute teacher, teacher aide, janitor, respiratory therapy technician, gas station attendant (when such things existed), salesclerk, writing instructor, and more not worth mentioning. He has been a full-time freelance writer since the mid-1980s, concentrating on fiction, nonfiction, and poetry. His hobbies include music and crafting Native American flutes. Please visit csfuqua.weebly.com and connect with him on Twitter and Facebook.

Books by C.S. Fuqua

Cancer
White Trash & Southern, Collected Poems, Volume I
Muscle Shoals ~ The Hit Capital's Heyday & Beyond
The Native American Flute: Myth, History, Craft
Hush, Puppy! A Southern Fried Tale
The Swing: Poems of Fatherhood
If I Were, I Would!
Notes to My Becca
Big Daddy's Fast-Past Gadget
Trust Walk
Rise Up
Deadlines audio novel series:
    Death in Service
    Deadlines
    Flight of the Omni
    Butterflies Die
Divorced Dads
Alabama Musicians: Musical Heritage from the Heart of Dixie
Music Fell on Alabama

CDs by C.S. Fuqua

WindPoem I ~ Native American Flute Meditations
WindPoem II ~ Native American Flute Meditations
WindPoem III ~ Native American Flute Meditations

Made in the USA
San Bernardino, CA
20 February 2016